PROST!

PROST!

The Story of German Beer

Horst D. Dornbusch

SIRIS BOOKS

A Division of

brewers
publications

Boulder, Colorado

Brewers Publications, Division of the Association of Brewers
PO Box 1679, Boulder, CO 80306-1679
(303) 447-0816; Fax (303) 447-2825

Printed in the United States of America
10 9 8 7 6 5 4 3 2 1

ISBN 0-937381-55-1

Library of Congress Cataloging-in-Publication Data
Dornbusch, Horst D.
    Prost! : the story of German beer / Horst D. Dornbusch.
      p. cm.
    Includes bibliographical references.
    ISBN 0-937381-55-1
    1. Beer—Germany—History. I. Title
TP577.D67 1997
641.2'3'0943—dc21   97-18237
                                                        CIP

Book Project Editor: Theresa Duggan
Copy Editor: Dianne Russell and Kathrin Rueda
Assistant Editor: Kim Adams
Art Director: Vicki Hopewell
Cover Designer: Liz Howe
Interior Designer: Ray Tollison
Interior illustrations by Mark Duffley unless otherwise noted.

Please direct all inquiries or orders to the above address.

To Kathrin.
She knows why.

Table of Contents

Foreword

■ ■

When I returned from my first trip to Germany in 1985, I knew I'd go back to Europe as soon as I graduated from college. My interest in brewing was waxing, and with the advent of some of the microbreweries in the Pacific Northwest, I decided that an education in brewing was my ticket back across the Atlantic. Unaware that England, France, Austria, and Belgium all have reputable brewing schools and degree programs, I looked only to Germany as the country where I would learn how to really make beer. I am now aware of the rich traditions and high-quality educational infrastructures other European brewing nations have, but ten years ago I intuitively made the right choice for me when I headed to Germany.

Every brewing nation in the world looks to Germany for brewing techniques and equipment, beer styles and ingredients, trained brewing personnel, nomenclature, glassware, and even beer itself. Building a reputation of such huge proportions is not something that develops overnight. *Prost!* is perhaps the only work in English that details how the political, economic, and social history of Germany are inextricably linked to its brewing history and culture. This work also clearly shows us how German brewing technology achieved critical mass in the nineteenth and twentieth centuries. Without the strong role beer played in German culture, the drive to develop brewing technology would not have existed. Without this technology German brewers would not have been able to grow, thrive, survive political and economic crises, and export this technology, as well as beer culture and tradition, to virtually every country in the world.

My knowledge of German beer culture and history has been won mostly in osmotic and piecemeal fashion. Although this is partially a result of my own somewhat unsystematic approach to learning, it is mainly attributable to the fact that until now there really hasn't been a book that lays out German brewing history from start to finish. Horst Dornbusch has taken the time to detail the development of German brewing from the days of the Germanic tribes to the present. Finally, there is an accurate, comprehensive overview of the history of beer and brewing in Germany that obviates the need to pore over volumes of dry history books, each of which may contain as little as one or two relevant bits about brewing.

What Dornbusch has done so brilliantly is to look at the development of beer traditions and culture on a regional basis. Any of us who can think back to our world history lessons will recall that Germany, relative to many other European powers, was late to unify and federalize politically and economically. Naturally, this acted as a preservative in allowing different regions to retain their unique cultural flavor. Far too often I hear people generalize about "German beer" and Dornbusch has shed light on the strong traditions that have evolved regionally in German brewing.

Prost! also provides us with many interesting tidbits on how beer styles, customs, cuisine, and traditions have developed in Germany. In addition, it provides the basics of brewing in order to place the brewing traditions and beer styles in context. The real beauty of Dornbusch's work is that it can be read and enjoyed by anyone interested in beer, history, and a well-written book. *Prost!* would even be an excellent adjunct to German history classes because it chronologically parallels German history and it shows what a tremendous impact brewing has had on German politics, economics, and custom.

Having lived and worked in Munich for four years, I consider myself fortunate to have been able to learn about German beer and brewing first-hand. Although I learned much during my stay there, Horst Dornbusch's *Prost!* edified me about the beer styles I love to drink, how they evolved, and what their place in world brewing history is. As a beer drinker I have come to appreciate the diversity of the world's beer styles, both commercial and obscure. As a brewer I have developed a curiosity for brewing techniques around the globe. Like a favorite restaurant you always go back to, I always instinctively come back to German beers and brewing techniques. *Prost!* reminds me of why I went to Germany to learn about beer in the first place.

Eric Warner
Owner of Tabernash Brewing Company

Preface

■■■■■■■■■■■■■■■■■■■■■■■■■■■■■■

Welcome to the world of German beer! German beers have been my passion ever since I can remember. To me, there is no better lubricant of social intercourse than a fine brew that is elegant in appearance and rich in flavor. A great German beer appeals to all the senses. It has a full-bodied mouthfeel with a delicate—not burpy—effervescence that percolates deliciously over the palate during an unhurried sip. It emanates a noble hop bouquet and sports a firm, creamy head. It is served not chilled but cool, and in a glass, not out of the bottle. O wondrous quaff from the humble grain!

When I think of beer, I am reminded of Friedrich Schiller's famous ode *Die Glocke* (The Bell), in which the poet describes the church bell as mankind's constant companion amid life's turbulent changes. The bell rings in the christening of a newborn, booms its ominous alert when disaster strikes, beckons a merry company to a wedding ceremony, and, finally, sounds a somber farewell when we are laid to rest. Beer is just such a constant companion, especially in Germany. There is no event in that country, grave or trivial, large or small, at which beer is not served. I wonder how much nonsense and how much profundity has been discussed through the ages over a glass of beer. Beer stimulates, beer affirms, beer consoles. German culture without beer is unthinkable.

When you sit down in a North American restaurant, the first gesture of welcome is a glass of water put before you. In Germany, a glass of the local brew is considered the proper way to start a meal. Often it appears before you even have a chance to order it. If you want water instead, you must ask for it.

In Germany, nobody is considered too young to have a taste of beer. Even children often get a glass of beer at the dinner table, usually a *malzbier,* a sweet, dark, low-alcohol-content brew. Many German physicians counsel expectant mothers to have a moderate amount of brew every day. Corporate cafeterias offer beer as a matter of course. There are even beer vending machines in most workplaces spitting out half-liter bottles for 1.50 marks. The kiosk at the local bus stop and the convenience store at the gas station sell not only newspapers, chewing gum, and cigarettes but also beer. At the time of this writing, the patent office in Munich is even considering an application to protect a recipe for beer jelly. This beery breakfast spread is available in Pils, weizen, and alt flavors.

Beer is a natural companion of life in Germany. It is considered one of the supreme earthly pleasures, and it is universally of high quality. It is not intended as a drug with which to get loaded, but as the proper default drink for any occasion. I have embraced that approach to beer. My motto: Drink less, drink better, and always enjoy. That's what this book is all about. Have fun learning about the past and the present of German beer, and may the knowledge of its tradition deepen your reverence for the truly unique achievement it represents.

Relax, raise your glass, have a good brew and a good read.
Prost!

Horst D. Dornbusch
Essex, Massachusetts

Introduction

■ ■

T his book is about the marvels and mysteries of German beer. On the face of it, beer—any beer—is a simple beverage: All you need is some malted grain, a good dose of water, a smidgen of flavorings, a bit of yeast, and, *voilà,* you've got beer.

It is the brewer's art, and a true art it is, that turns these simple materials into an endless variety of divine gustatory pleasures. Germany's twelve hundred or so breweries make more than five thousand different beers in about a dozen major styles, all from the same basic ingredients. There is a lot for us to explore and to savor!

Beverages are symbols of cultural achievement. The great ones are pearls of civilization that have matured over centuries. When we think of Champagne, cabernet sauvignon, or Cognac, for instance, we conjure up images of the *joie de vivre* of the French. When we savor a sherry or a Malaga, we are partaking in the mystery that is southern Spain. How could a frozen vodka be anything but Russian or a tequila anything but Mexican? Likewise, when we drink a Munich helles or an Oktoberfest beer, we are vicariously transported into the *lederhosen*-slapping land of the Bavarians. The character of the drink seems always a reflection of the character of the people who created it.

Germany and England—
The Great Beer Cultures

Ask anyone anywhere about the greatest cuisines of the world and invariably the answer will point to the culinary contributions made by France, Italy, and China, though not always in that order. To be sure, there are other interesting cuisines, such as Japanese, Indian, and Greek, but none have achieved the overall subtlety and complexity of the three famous

culinary cultures. Now ask the same question about beer. The answer will undoubtedly lead you to Germany and England. This is not to say that the Belgians and the Scandinavians, for instance, have not made their contributions to the history of beer, but no people has produced such a variety, complexity, and quality of brews as have the Germans and the English.

Let's be politically incorrect: When we refer to English beers, we mean all the beers brewed by the English method. Those include the beers of Scotland, Wales, and Ireland—they are all part of the same brewing tradition. Likewise, when we refer to German beers, we are not limiting ourselves to the current geographical boundaries of the Federal Republic. Rather, we are referring to all the ancient and recent beer styles that have sprung from the regional brewing traditions of central Europe. German-style beers are also brewed in the Czech Republic (Bohemia), Austria, Switzerland, France, Scandinavia, Belgium, Holland, and in North and South America.

The British Isles are home to rich, fruity, complex ales with great variations in color and bitterness. There is pale ale, amber ale, red ale, brown ale, bitter, extra special bitter (ESB), India pale ale (IPA), barley wine, dark ale, porter, Scotch ale, and stout. A clean bitterness with fruity overtones characterizes the flavor profile of these ales. Their malty notes increase as the color deepens from pale to dark. Darker ales also exhibit toasty, roasted flavors from the high-temperature kilning of the darker malt varieties. Because English beers are fermented relatively warm with fast-acting yeast strains, buttery notes are acceptable.

The German tradition has spawned an equally stunning variety of both ales and lagers. There is alt, kölsch, weizen, Berliner weisse, dunkelweizen, bock, doppelbock, Vienna, Märzen, Oktoberfest, helles,

Bohemian Pilsner, Pils or Pilsener, Dortmunder export, rauchbier, and schwarzbier. Their flavor profiles change as you travel from north to south. Whereas sharper, hoppier, more pungent notes predominate in beers brewed close to the sea, mellow, malty notes are most evident in beers brewed closer to the Alps. As a general rule, maltiness increases as color deepens, but toastiness is considered an off-flavor in German beers, even in the darker brews. Fermented with slow-acting yeasts at relatively low temperatures and aged near the freezing point for two weeks to several months, German beers are always mellow and clean-tasting. Buttery notes are unacceptable.

In the Beginning There Was Ale

It may come as a surprise to modern beer enthusiasts that the history of German beer has been for the most part one of ale, not of lager—

in spite of the present-day preponderance of blonde lagers, which currently hold well over two-thirds of the German beer market. But if you scratch the surface of the German lager veneer, what you'll find is a bedrock of solid ale traditions. Until the sixteenth century, all German beer was ale. Until about the eighth century it was brewed almost exclusively in the home, by tribal *hausfrauen*. By the eleventh century it was brewed mostly by professional brewmonks and brewnuns until feudal lords took over most institutional brewing in southern Germany. Burgher-merchants did the same in northern Germany.

Germans have been brewing ales for at least three thousand years but lagers (specifically brown lagers) for only five centuries. The blonde, crisp, clean lagers for which Germans have become so famous in our age have been around for a scant 150 years. The now ubiquitous hoppy Pils started its conquest only about thirty years ago. Thus, do not judge history by

Sign at the entrance of a 1378 watering hole in Celle, in Lower Saxony, where city councilors used to discuss politics over tankards of ale.

the most recent past, lest you take as fact what might be a fad or a short-term trend. Decades, even centuries, do not mean all that much in a country where a traveler can eat and drink in places that were already old when Columbus sailed the seas and discovered there was an entire continent blocking his route to the Orient. There are pubs in Germany where centuries of stolid bums have rubbed cozy, indelible hollows into wooden benches from which a contemporary imbiber can take unobtrusive support and comfort as he settles in for an evening of delectable degustation.

Beer, Politics, Economics, and Religion

In Germany, the fortunes of beer have always been intimately intertwined with the ups and downs of the country's political and religious history, but the secular and the sacred have been strange bedfellows, each with the capacity to reach down into the everyday life of the common man and to regulate everyone's existence from cradle to grave.

The secular authorities build roads, collect taxes, train armies, mete out justice, mint coins, finance welfare, and organize the police, and the churches preach morals, baptize babies, bury the dead, set up schools and hospitals, and give to the poor. But at certain times in history, religious leaders, in competition with their secular counterparts, also had their own armies, sources of tax revenue, courts of law, territorial claims, and commercial enterprises.

What does this have to do with German beer, you may ask? The answer is: Everything! In a culture where beer partly defines the national character, the question of who controls the brew is paramount. He who has his hand on the levers of power also has his thumb in the people's beer mug.

One can trace the roots of German beer making back to the tribal Germanic marauders of yore. These inhabitants of the dark Teutonic forests used to menace the poor Roman legionnaires who were sent to the region to do Caesar's bidding. As we know from Roman reports, Germanic *hausfrau* brewsters minded the kettle in the forest clearings. Yes, home brewing had been a venerable tradition on this earth long before February 1979, when President Jimmy Carter repealed its prohibition in the United States.

Between the sixth and the ninth centuries, the tribal societies of central Europe became both Christianized and organized into countries united by language and customs. This set the stage for a power struggle between the secular feudal lords and the Christian bishops and monks for control over all facets of life—including beer making! By the eleventh century monastic breweries, run mostly by Benedictine monks and nuns, enjoyed an almost exclusive right to brew and sell beer. By the twelfth century, the feudal nobility, possessed by greed and envy and always strapped for money, began to

Wood carving in the Küppers Museum in Cologne depicting a brew monk.

take back most of the brew privileges they had granted to the religious orders during the previous centuries. Many a lord started his own *Hofbräuhaus* (court brew house).

When the struggle between the feudal lords and the clerics over the spoils of power was at its most ferocious, both parties seemed to have missed the rise, at the beginning of the second millennium, of a new, third force in society, which was ultimately to snatch the economic prize out of their clutches. This emerging force was the enterprising city burghers, who quietly created a new prosperity based on industry, commerce, and technological innovation. Within a few centuries the merchant class had all but monopolized the making of top-quality beers that tasted great and kept well. This class erected private trading empires that spanned most of the known world of the time, and beer, next to minerals, furs, and dry goods was among its most profitable commodities. Through their commercial ventures, these free-spirited burghers planted the seeds of our modern civilization and would, in due course, limit the clergy to its spiritual purpose and relegate the nobles to the historical junk heap.

The development of German beer as we know it today was virtually finished by the time the twentieth century rolled around—as were the struggles for political and economic power between church and state and between the common people and the aristocrats. But for about a thousand years the question of who ran the country and owned the beer—monks, lords, merchants, or guilds—had determined which beers were brewed and distributed where, in which quantity, and of which quality. Church, state, and free enterprise each had its fair share in either furthering or retarding the progress of German beer. From their literally murky beginnings at the dawn of European civilization, German beers have evolved into mature, sophisticated brews with an unmistakable character that stems from a unique combination of ingredients and processes.

This book is about that evolution. It sheds light on the obvious and not so obvious historical forces and cultural traditions that have shaped German beers in all their variety over the centuries and highlights the differences between the beer styles that have come down to us as a result. Let this book take you on a journey of discovery so that the next time you pop open a bottle of German beer you can savor not only its sublime complexity but also the story behind it.

Five-Hundred-Year Milestones of German History and Beer

Bronze Age Brewing from 2000 to 1000 B.C.

Nordic sagas, which were not written down until two thousand years after this period, give hints of brewing as an everyday affair even at the dawn of central European civilization.

1000 to 500 B.C.

Beer making becomes standardized. Half-baked loaves of bread mixed with water produce a murky, turbid ale. A burial site near Kulmbach, Bavaria, dating from about 800 B.C. reveals earliest archaeological evidence of German beer making.

500 B.C. to Birth of Christ

The first Roman contact with northern European tribes yields descriptions of German beer making. German beer making evolves from bread-loaf mashing to grain mashing.

Birth of Christ to A.D. 500

Tribal *hausfrau* brewing flourishes during the Roman occupation, and the Romans set up their own breweries. The Roman empire eventually weakens and is smashed by invading Germans.

A.D. 500 to 1000

During the Dark Ages society stagnates north of the Alps, but the feudal state and the Christian church build large breweries and turn brewing into a profession. Brewmonks and nuns propel beer quality to hitherto unknown heights.

A.D. 1000 to 1500

The first German empire is constituted (it was to last for more than eight centuries). The Dark Ages are over, and cities grow. The monks lose their brewrights, and feudal lords in southern Germany make generally bad beer. However, city burghers in northern Germany make excellent beer, which they sell all over Europe.

A.D. 1500 to 1900

The Reformation and the Thirty Years' War destroy northern German beer making, but the beer purity law (*Reinheitsgebot)* rescues beer making in Bavaria. Science unravels the mysteries of fermentation. Technology provides process control in the brew house. Southern Germany specializes in lagers, and northern Germany continues to make ales.

Today

Both north and south make great lagers and ales. The *Reinheitsgebot* governs beer making (and taxation) in all of Germany. The number of large breweries is declining because of corporate mergers, but small brewpubs are experiencing a resurgence in popularity.

chapter 1

The Dawn of German Beer

■ ■

*T*he tribal inhabitants of northern and central Europe started to make beer from wheat, barley, or any other grain that grew wild and was not considered much use for anything else as early as the latter part of the Bronze Age, probably before 1000 B.C. This we know from the ancient sagas and myths. At that time, Celtic and Germanic tribes were competing for control over patches of inhabitable space in the forests. The struggle between the two groups lasted until about the fourth century B.C., when the Germans had either ousted the Celts from the continent or had assimilated them. Only in the British Isles and along the Atlantic coast of present-day France did the Celts remain the dominant cultural force for another millennium or so.

The tribes of central Europe, spread out over such a large territory and with very little communication among them, naturally were less homogeneous than the collective term "German" implies. The Danes, Norwegians, and Swedes of Scandinavia evolved their distinct Norse culture, and the inhabitants of Caesar's *Gallia* (roughly modern France and Belgium) developed their Gallic ways. Only the tribes in the very center—prominent among them the Alemans, Swabians, Bavarians, and Saxons—created a culture that we now associate with the term "German." But no matter where the Germans lived and what their customs, they were brewers all.

The pagans of northern Europe called their beer *öl,* which is the root of the modern word "ale." But because these folk could neither read nor write, we have no firm documentary evidence of the beginnings of their ale. We do know for sure, however, that the Germans were already regular ale brewers by about 800 B.C. Archaeologists have uncovered the burial site of a well-to-do German of that time near the Franconian village of Kasendorf, seven miles from Kulmbach in northern Bavaria. The

Coaster of EKU Pils from the northern Bavarian town of Kulmbach. Around 800 B.C., a gentleman was buried near there with crocks of beer. These crocks are the earliest archeological evidence of beer making in Germany.

grave not only contained the remains of the deceased gentleman but also the provisions his contemporaries had generously supplied for his trip into the realm of the spirits. Among these were crocks of beer, which, when unearthed almost three thousand years later, still contained traces of bread—the standard raw material for the mashes of ancient times.

Today, Kulmbach is home to many famous brews, including the Kulmbacher Mönchshof Kloster Schwarzbier, a malty black lager. Founded as a monastery brewery in 1349 and secularized in 1791, the Mönchshof brewery is still going strong as part of the Kulmbacher Reichelbräu conglomerate. Surely, almost three thousand years of virtually uninterrupted brewing in the Kulmbach region must constitute a world record!

Early beers were usually dark brews "mashed" from half-baked loaves of bread that was made from coarsely ground barley or wheat. The gentle, moist baking of the loaves probably had a similar effect on the grain to today's malting: that is, of activating the enzymes required for the conversion of starches into fermentable sugars. This "modified" bread was then soaked in crocks filled with water, where it fermented. The result was a murky and sour ale full of floating husks and crumbs—a far cry from the clean and crisp beers made in Germany today.

The first truly historical accounts of beer making among the Germans came from their Roman conquerors—those literate, wine-drinking military men and imperial officials who reveled in exposing the deplorable predilection of the barbarian *Germanii* for their inferior "barley wines"

Beer Fit for the Gods

What the northern tribes lacked in written records they made up for in oral folklore. Most famous among their stories are the *Edda,* a collection of old Norse mythological stories, and the *Kalevala,* a more modern collection based on old Finnish mythology. These sagas depict events that occurred well before the birth of Christ and Roman contact and were preserved in the oral tradition. This is why the Nordic tales were written down for the first time as late as the eleventh century. The sagas sing of the daily life of the pagan tribes and their gods and of the brews they made. Beer had always been a keystone of the Germanic culture.

In the *Kalevala,* which has four hundred verses about beer making but only two hundred about the creation of the world (how is that for priorities?), we find a poetic description of the tumultuous process we now call fermentation:

> Heatedly moves the beer in oaken barrels,
> and vehemently curses the brew.

We also learn that beer making was women's work:

> Now the beer is finished,
> ready for the men to drink

> Carefully and with skill
> has the wife and hostess
> readied the beer for us,
> and the sweet refreshment flows
> from the sweetly spiced malt.

There is even a reference to lagering:

> The red beer was stored,
> the light beer was kept,
> in the earth to sleep. (Hellex 1981)

The *Edda* is an epos populated with heroic beer drinkers. There is King Hedric, the dwarf Alvis, and, of course, Odin, the guardian of Valhalla and father of the Valkyries, the equestrian maidens who reward all slain heroes with beer for their valiant deeds in battle. Even in death, beer can be a great comfort, as we learn from the dying King Regnar, who laughs away his final hours in joyful anticipation of the first draft of good beer in the beyond.

The Nordic and Germanic peoples considered the sky a giant brew kettle, and when Thor, the god of thunder, cleaned and polished the kettle, all mortals knew about it. On days when he brewed, there were clouds in the sky.

Beer was revered as a godly drink that commands respect. The *Edda* admonishes not to "get glued to the mug, but to drink beer in moderation," for beer can "lame one person's whit, while spur another's tongue." Hence Odin's pearl of wisdom: "Stick to your mead, but mind your measure, so that you know when to speak and when to keep silent" (Hellex 1981).

A Nordic drinking vessel. This one is from Island and dates from around 1500 A.D.

(Hellex 1981). These, by Roman standards, were second-rate beverages, often flavored with such unspeakables as oak bark, aspen leaves, or even the content of an ox's gall bladder.

At the time of the first Roman contact, the Germans were already producing beer in large quantities. Thus wrote the Greco-Roman geographer Strabo (around 63 B.C.–A.D. 21), when he reported that one tribe, the Cimbri, used bronze brew kettles capable of holding about 500 liters. Today we would call this a 4½-barrel brew house. A remarkable metallurgical achievement for that time (Lohberg n.d.)!

Some historians speculate that Julius Caesar and his legions learned about beer making from the Germans and introduced it to the British Isles in 55 or 53 B.C., but other historians insist that the Celts had mastered the art of ale making on their own long before the Romans figured out how to cross the British Channel in boats. Suffice it to say that around the birth of Christ, ale was the most popular drink of the Europeans north of the Alps.

Eins, Zwei, G'suffa . . . Two Thousand Years Ago

The best description of tribal Germanic drinking habits has come to us from the Roman historian Publius Cornelius Tacitus. In his *De Origine et Situ Germanorum* (About the Origin and Location of the Germans), which he completed in A.D. 98, Tacitus asserted, with some contempt, that

the Germanic folk were proficient imbibers who sought out the slightest excuse for having a drinking party. No other people, he wrote, were inclined to enjoy so much the art of banqueting and entertaining as the Germans, and it was customary for them to invite strangers into their homes to share a meal and a brew. "The *Germanii*," he wrote, "serve an extract of barley and rye as a beverage that is somehow adulterated [presumably he means fermented] to resemble wine" (Hellex 1981). Perhaps the cartoon cliché of raucous tribesmen frolicking on their bear skins in front of a campfire and passing, from one eager mouth to the next, richly ornamented aurochs horns filled with intoxicating liquids is not too far-fetched after all.

Tacitus was impressed by the vigor and energy of the Germans. He described the country as rough and crude and the air as unpleasant, but the people as pure and unspoiled. He observed that the men were capable of withstanding cold and hunger and were always ready to attempt feats of daring. There was one deprivation, however, the Germans apparently could not bear: thirst! No wonder that both honey beer (mead) and grain beer always flowed in copious quantities at important tribal gatherings, where the Germans discussed such weighty matters as war and peace or the betrothal of a chieftain's daughter.

The Germans knew how to have fun and, contrary to current perceptions of their twentieth-century descendants, were none too eager to do heavy work. At least this is what Tacitus wanted us to believe. He even suggested that it might have been easier to conquer the *Germanii* by shipments of *cerevisia* (beer) than by force of *pilum* (lance) and *gladius* (sword): "If we wanted to make use of their addiction to drink, by giving them as much of it as they want, we could defeat them as easily

A German tribesman (center) raises a toast with a drinking
vessel made from an aurochs horn.

An aurochs.

This is what a German tribal beer stein looked like before it was removed from its original
owner, the aurochs. The hollow horns of this bovine served as handy drinking vessels to
the German tribesmen. The aurochs is the ancestor of all domestic cattle. The last wild spec-
imens of this critter were seen in the forests of Poland. Extinct for about 350 years, the
aurochs has now been back-crossed by German zoologists. As a supplier of beer containers, fortunately, the aurochs has been replaced by modern glass and earthenware factories.

by means of this vice as with our weapons . . . They cultivate the grains
of the field with much greater patience and perseverance than one would
expect from them, in light of their customary laziness" (Hellex 1981).

Gallic Beers with Flavor

To the Romans, things appeared not much different on the other
side of the Rhine. In present-day France, where the Gallic tribes lived, the
Roman traveler Pytheas observed around 440 B.C. that "beer is the most
common beverage among the Gallic peoples." Likewise, the statesman
Marcus Porcius Cato (234–149 B.C.) remarked in his *De Agricultura* (On
Agriculture) that beer was the national beverage of the Gauls. Pliny the
Elder, who died in Pompeii during the Vesuvius eruption of A.D. 79, confirmed that "the Gaul generally drinks barley wine, as he always has, and
he understands how to brew different varieties, with which he gets ine-
briated." The Gauls sometimes flavored their beers with caraway or, if
they could afford it, with honey (Hellex 1981).

The End of Rome—At the Hands of Ale-Drinking Barbarians

Attila the Hun: Make love not war—a curious twist on a familiar theme.

Not only libationarily but militarily as well, Roman finesse turned out to be no match for Germanic resolve. The first serious blow to Roman dominance in central Europe occurred as early as A.D. 9, in the Teuteburg Forest, southeast of present-day Bielefeld in the state of North Rhine–Westphalia. There, a band of warriors from the Cheruscan tribe, lead by their chief, Arminius, massacred Emperor Augustus's entire occupation force in Germany. The Cheruscans completely vanquished the emperor's three legions of about six thousand men each. The rout was so disastrous that Publius Quintilius Varus, the general in charge, committed suicide after the defeat rather than return to Rome and face Augustus's wrath.

Over the next few centuries, successive waves of ale-drinking northern barbarians forayed into the vast reaches of the empire amassed by the civilized, wine-drinking Romans. The Germanic Visigoths, on the move with women, children, elders, and young horsemen-warriors, crossed the lower Danube in A.D. 376 and destroyed a Roman army near Constantinople (present-day Istanbul). Later, under their famous leader Alaric I, they swept through Greece and Italy. By A.D. 410 they had reached the gates of the city of Rome itself, and the city experienced the first of many sackings at the hands of the barbarians. It finally was curtains for the *Pax Romana* (Roman Peace).

Attila and his Mongolian Huns came next and laid siege to the city. Rome got a miraculous reprieve, however, in 453, when Attila—quite literally—overdid his amorous exertions. He died, in flagrante, on a hot and steamy night, from an arterial hemorrhage while atop his favorite slave girl—a curious twist on the familiar theme: Make love not war. The Huns, now leaderless, inexplicably raised the siege, left Italy for good, and dispersed.

With the Germanic Vandals, who came by ship in 455, Rome was not so lucky. Unable to mount a defense, the city was completely ransacked during a two-week rampage. This is the origin of the English word "vandalize."

The Roman Empire had become a dying, impotent colossus, and entire peoples moved in from the outside to settle on its lands. The German Franks started to nibble on the giant's extremities in present-day Belgium, and the Burgundians crossed the Rhine to occupy what we still call Burgundy today. The Germanic Lombards, or *Langobardi* (long beards), moved from their home in the lands beyond the Danube into northern Italy, where, in the 570s, they established a flourishing society around Pavia in what we still call Lombardy. In Gaul, Clovis (circa 466–511), leader of the Salish Franks, finished off Syagrius, the last Roman general there. Known in history by his gallicized name, Louis I, the first king of France, Clovis then subdued all the tribes between the Pyrenees and Bavaria and made Paris the capital of his new realm.

After a thousand years of glory, the Roman Empire finally collapsed. Several centuries of turmoil followed, during which Europe was pilfered and pillaged by invading vagabonds from all directions of the compass. Viking raiders, probably driven by population pressures, descended Europe's northern and western coastlines in their dragon-headed, flat-bottomed, open longboats, the *knorr,* and raised hell and pandemonium up and down the continent's major rivers, reaching as far inland as Paris and Cologne. To the east, Magyar horsemen, following in the hoofprints of the Huns, looted and burned villages from the Elbe to the Loire. To the south, seafaring Saracens from the Arab caliphate that used to be the Roman province of Africa terrorized the coastal regions of the Mediterranean. Using their pirate's nest of Le Freinet, near present-day Saint-Tropez in France, as a base, the Saracens staged raids into the hinterland, terrorizing settlements and mountain passes as far from the sea as the high Alps in present-day Switzerland. They even helped themselves to free beer at the famous brew monastery of Saint Gall.

The empire founded by Clovis was to expand under his successors during the next three hundred years until it encompassed all of continental Europe from Hamburg to Rome. Only upon the death of Charlemagne's son, Louis the Pious, in 840, was the empire to be subdivided into three parts, the Kingdom of West Francia under Charles the Bald, the Middle Kingdom under Lothar I, and the Kingdom of East Francia under Louis the German. The west and east kingdoms, respectively, eventually became the empires of France and Germany, whereas the Middle Kingdom, composed of Lotharingia, Burgundy, Provence, Lombardy, and Spoleto, was gradually absorbed by the other two.

On the culinary and linguistic front, France, after the division of central Europe into three kingdoms in the ninth century, preserved the Roman influences perhaps more so than did Germany and went largely its own, mostly wine-drinking way, while, on the other side of the Rhine, beer making gradually rose from an everyday household chore to a fine art and a serious economic and political affair.

True order returned to central Europe only during the tenth century, this time with a medieval Germanic touch. In one of those ironies of history, the new empire, feudal and Christian, called itself the Holy Roman Empire of the German Nation. It was formed in 962 and combined all the lands from Sicily to the North Sea under one ruler, the Saxon strongman, Otto I.

This empire was so vast that it proved politically ungovernable. Yet it lasted for almost nine hundred years before it died an inglorious death in 1806, when, after centuries of regional and religious strife, the Austrian occupier of the throne, Francis II, simply renounced the crown. In spite of its political instability, this empire provided the social framework for a millennium of German brewing history during which German beers ascended from their primitive tribal beginnings to the crisp, clean ales and lagers they are today.

A Bouquet of Billy Goat

In Roman high society German beer was held in such disdain that even Emperor Flavius Claudius Julianus (A.D. 331–363) felt himself called upon to rhyme a silly ditty about the superior virtues of wine as compared to beer. In his poem, he likened the smell of wine to that of nectar and the smell of the Germanic "drink from grain" to that of a billy goat. Julianus had come to know the Germans and their beer from his many battles against the Franks and Alemans (Hellex 1981).

Unimpressed by the highbrow Roman attitude, however, the tribal marauders of the Gallic and Teutonic forests continued to down their native beverages just as they continued to menace the poor legionnaires sent from the Apennine Peninsula to keep an eye on them. The sylvan primitives proved to be intrepid warriors who were as fond of draining the lifeblood out of their sophisticated wine-drinking oppressors as they were of draining their aurochs horns of murky quaff. For the emissaries of mighty Rome, life was never safe at such camps as *Colonia Claudia Ara Agrippinensium* (today's Cologne), *Castra Novesia* (today's Neuß, outside Düsseldorf), *Castra Xantippa* (today's Xanten, on the Rhine near the Dutch border), or *Treveris* (today's Trier at the Moselle River, near Luxembourg).

If You Can't Lick Them, Join Them

The Romans had brought the grape to central Europe so that they could indulge in the drinking habits to which they were accustomed at home. But it is obvious that eventually they developed a taste for the "inferior" beverage of their Germanic underlings. How else are we to interpret the tombstone of a Roman merchant, who died in *Treveris* on the Moselle River in A.D. 260? The epitaph on his stone identifies him as a *cervesarius,* a beer merchant. Founded by Emperor Augustus in 15 B.C., *Treveris* was the capital of the western part of the Roman Empire and served as administrative headquarters of the Roman territories from Spain to Britain. In this great city, our *cervesarius* had his liquid wares privately brewed by German women in the neighborhood and sold the merchandise at a fine markup to his civilized Roman customers.

The Romans even learned to brew themselves, as is evident from a complete Roman brewery discovered in 1983 near the Bavarian city of

Regensburg on the banks of the Danube. This brewery dates from the second or third century A.D. and was part of a *canaba,* a settlement of craftsmen, that had sprung up within the walls of a fortification called *Castra Regina* (hence the modern name of the city: Regensburg). *Castra Regina* was built in A.D. 179 by the Roman emperor Marcus Aurelius. Because of its strategic location along the northeastern flank of the empire, it became the largest Roman camp in what is now southern Germany, housing some six thousand obviously thirsty legionnaires, as well as scores of administrators and support personnel.

Tombstone fragment of a *cervesarius,* a Roman beer merchant who died in the Moselle valley in 260 A.D.

It is apparent from the construction of the kiln and mash tun of the ancient Regensburg brewery that German beer making had, by that time, progressed from the primitive bread beer found in the grave near Kulmbach to the mashing of malted grains as we practice it today.

Evidence of another Roman brewery in Germany, a fermenter with residues of black beer, was found in 1911 during the excavation of a Roman camp near Alzey, in Germany's largest wine-growing region, in the state of Rhineland-Palatine. Apparently, the fermenter and its contents were hastily abandoned by the Romans sometime in the year A.D. 353 during a surprise attack by the Alemans.

The Romans' ultimate embrace of the barbaric beverage is also reflected in their language. They came to regard beer as a gift from Ceres, the goddess of agriculture, and treasured it as a strength-giving potion. Hence their word for beer: *cerevisia (vis* means strength).

chapter 2

Elsewhere in the Ancient World . . .

A round of beer in Sumeria about 3100 B.C. This is the oldest known picture of beer drinking in the world.

Nobody knows for sure where and when it all started. Its dawn is shrouded in obscurity, but the consensus among anthropologists and archaeologists is that brewing probably evolved independently at separate points of the globe rather than at a single location. The Chinese have known how to make rice beer for thousands of years. Indian brewsters in Peru made *chicha,* a corn beer, long before the Spaniards arrived there. African tribes made beer from millet. The northern and central European tribes started making beer from wheat and barley in the Bronze Age probably no later than 1000 B.C.

The world's very first brewers, however, were most likely early Stone Age inhabitants of the Middle East. Experts surmise that they discovered beer making by accident perhaps some ten thousand years ago. A forgetful baker—probably the woman of the house or her maid—might have left the dough out during a rainstorm. When the rays of the returning sun warmed the earthenware mixing bowl, it became a combination mash tun and open fermenter in which the grain's enzymes, together with airborne yeasts, converted the dough's starches into sugars and sugars into alcohol. Perhaps out of innate curiosity, the baker tasted the ale she had inadvertently concocted and appreciated the sour, refreshing taste— and perhaps the heady aftereffect as well. There must have been deliberate attempts to replicate the accidental dough brew.

Sumerian Brews—The First on Record

By about 4000 B.C., a complex and literate agrarian society had emerged in Mesopotamia between the rivers Euphrates and Tigris, within the borders of present-day Iraq. These people called themselves Sumerians, and they had a highly sophisticated beer culture.

Their brews were made from *emmer* (a speltlike wheat), barley, or a combination of the two grains.

The epos of the Sumerian king Gilgamesh, mankind's oldest known piece of literature, written in hieroglyphs on twelve tablets toward the end of the third millennium B.C., reveals that the Sumerians were well acquainted with beer's transformative effects:

> The wild beast Enkidu drank beer. He drank of it seven times. His spirit relaxed and he started to talk in a loud voice. Well-being filled his body and his face turned bright. He washed his matted fleece with water and rubbed his body with oil, and Enkidu became human. (Hellex 1981)

In short, it's beer that makes us human. The Sumerian tablets are now in the Louvre in Paris.

The Sumerians, because of the records they left behind, were the world's first recognized ale drinkers. To them, beer had a humanizing influence; indeed, it defined man. It gentled the savage qualities of the mystical half-man half-bull brute Enkidu, thus serving as the midwife of civilization.

Beer consumption among the Sumerians was high. Almost half the region's annual harvest of wheat and barley went into brewing. Brewing, practiced by both women and men, became a respectable profession. Brewers (as well as cooks) attained great social rank and were even exempt from military service.

Communal beer drinking accompanied all great social occasions in old Mesopotamia, especially funerals. Sumerian tombstones depict servants offering beer to the gods to curry favor for the departed souls in the afterlife. The priests, who helped the souls make their transition to the beyond, in accordance

The world's oldest known piece of literature, a Sumerian tablet from the third millenium B.C. already talks about beer.

Slacking a thirst Babylonian-style about 4,000 years ago.

with established ritual were paid in bread and beer for their ceremonial services. According to a hieroglyphic find dating from 2900 B.C., a funeral cost seven urns of beer, a price that was later reduced to three urns as a result of popular discontent. It appears that the spiritual guardians of society, from the priests of Mesopotamia to the bacchantes of Rome and the monastics of medieval Europe, have always shown a great predilection for the fermented beverage.

The Babylonians Invent Beer Regulations

By about 2000 B.C., Babylonians had invaded the lands between the Euphrates and Tigris and, like all good conquerors, had usurped the achievements of the vanquished for themselves. Not only did the Babylonians continue the Sumerian tradition of making beer, but they added a novelty of their own: They invented beer regulation.

The Babylonians created definitions for twenty different beer styles, eight of which were made from barley. There was wheat beer, thin beer, red beer, black beer, and even a lagered beer for export, mostly to Egypt.

Beer regulations, as well as other laws, were severe in Babylon, as is evident from the legal code of King Hammurabi (circa 1750 B.C.), all 360 paragraphs of which were chiseled into a seven-foot-high diorite column that is now in the Louvre in Paris. Hammurabi decreed that a brewster who waters down her beer is to be drowned in it, and an innkeeper who tolerates political debates in her establishment must be put to death.

In Old Egypt, Beer Is Cash

The Egyptians, after being turned on to brewing by the Babylonians, elevated beer to the level of a true food commodity. In fact, the old Egyptian hieroglyph for meal is a compound of those for bread and beer. The Egyptians called their beer *kash,* from which the modern word "cash" derives, and used it as currency to pay slaves, tradesmen, priests, and public officials alike. None other than the god Osiris was hailed as the inventor of beer, and the craft of brewing, centered in the trading port of Pelusium at the mouth of the Nile, became big business.

An Egyptian Sweetheart Invents the Beer Tax

Beer had become so popular in ancient Egypt that no pharaoh dared to put a tax on it. Egyptians had to pay taxes *in* beer, never *on* beer, that is, until Cleopatra's clan, the Ptolemies, took over. Darling Cleo (69–30 B.C.) wanted to build more pyramids in her beloved Egypt, and for that she needed more cash. Thus, she is credited with the dubious achievement of having invented both the alcohol tax and its most perennial and insincere justification: to curb public drunkenness. Sound familiar? After Cleopatra, things went downhill for the Ptolemies, but the beer tax genie could never be put back into the bottle.

Cleopatra's Enduring Legacy

Ever since Cleopatra, governments have been able to find ways to cash in on things common folk like, and that disease is universal. In Germany, the first known local beer tax was instituted in the city of Ulm in 1220. The brewers and drinkers of Kulmbach in Bavaria got theirs in 1388, when the town's feudal lord, Margrave Friederich VI, came up with a "tap penny" and a "drink tax." He decreed that "people in the city and in the country pay for every keg one guilder in tax" (Hellex 1981). That was more money than most people earned in a day.

Does she look like she is enjoying her beer (tax)?

The great regulatory innovators and Bavarian corulers, the dukes Wilhelm IV and Ludwig X, best known for having mandated universal beer purity for all of Bavaria (in 1516), also have a less honorable achievement to their credit: They came up with the first universal Bavarian beer tax, which they instituted in 1543, allegedly to finance their wars against the Turks, although no army was ever raised. In due time the Turkish threat subsided, but the beer tax stayed!

Today, both accomplishments of the famous duo live on: in the purity of the beer that we enjoy and in the financial punishment we suffer as we enjoy. Their innovations are codified in the *Biersteuergesetz*, the German beer tax law. The famous beer purity law *(Reinheitsgebot)*, though initially intended to regulate only the *ingredients* of beer, is now simply a subchapter of the beer tax law.

Brewers in the United States have not fared much better. In fact, the U.S. institution that is charged with issuing brewers' licenses and regulating beer labels, the Bureau of Alcohol, Tobacco and Firearms, is not, as one would expect, part of the Department of Agriculture, the government agency that regulates the safety of our food. Instead, it is part of the Department of the Treasury, the agency that takes our money. Besides, what does beer have to do with guns? We can find no more telling statement about regulatory priorities!

Cleo set a trend that survived the rise and fall of many a civilization. It has known no national boundaries, no cultural barriers, no limits of time. *Plus ça change, plus c'est la même chose!*

Greek Beer Drinkers Fall on Their Backs

Ancient civilization, as we learn in our history books, was centered around the Mediterranean, which Plato in his *Phaedo* likened to a pond: ". . . the earth is a very large place, but we . . . live in only one small part of it, around the sea, like frogs around a pond" (Bloch 1991).

Greek beer mug from about 700 B.C.

It is likely that the Greeks first learned about beer through their contact with the Egyptians. There were Greek attempts at making beer, especially in the province of Thrace. On the whole, however, beer did not catch on in the cradle of Western civilization, probably because the climate and soil were more suitable for the cultivation of grapes and olives rather than grains. Thus, it is surprising that Aristotle (384–322 B.C.) had a kind word to say about beer drinkers: "Those who get drunk on beer, fall on their backs and lie with their faces up, while those who get drunk on wine fall down every which way" (Lohberg, n.d.).

Politically, it was the Romans who ruled this world around a pond. Between roughly 500 B.C. and the birth of Christ, they began to venture into the unknown corners of this "very large place." They called the new lands of dense forests north of the Alps *Germania*. There they encountered a separate—and to them barbaric—culture whose culinary life seemed to be centered around beer. It took the winedrinkers from the Mediterranean about five centuries to conquer the ale-drinking, illiterate savages, and then another five centuries to be conquered by them.

Beer Dies in the Middle East but Lives in Central Europe

Eventually, the center of quality brewing in the Old World shifted from the Middle East to central and northern Europe, apparently without any direct contact between the two beer cultures. Though Egyptian brewing continued to flourish until the eighth century A.D., it eventually fell victim to the abstemious zeal of a new religion. As the wave of Islam engulfed the Middle East, the Koran became law. And the Koran says that holy warriors shall practice sobriety. In order for beer to make it in that world, it was up to the tribal societies north of the Alps to bear the torch.

chapter 3

Of *Hausfrau* Brewsters, Vassals, Monks, and Nuns

■ ■ ■ ■ ■ ■ ■ ■ ■ ■ ■ ■ ■ ■ ■ ■ ■ ■ ■

Wﬁe are now peeking into the sixth century A.D. The Roman Empire had crumbled and the Germanic way of life flourished in the clearings of the Teutonic forests and along the riverbanks. For the next three centuries, life, when not interrupted by raiding Huns, Vikings, or Saracens, would generally be peaceful in the little farming villages up and down the lands of the Franks, Alemans, Saxons, Swabians, Thuringians, and Bavarians. Indigenous civilizations, no longer under the yoke of Latin legions and their *Pax Romana,* began to take shape.

While the man of the house was out tending his fields of barley and wheat or chasing the stag in the woods, the woman of the house was busy at the hearth making the bread, the stew, and the brew. In German families of that period, home brewing was as ubiquitous as home cooking and baking, and the brew kettle was as important a part of a maiden's dowry as were her cooking pots and pans. It was customary for a brewster *hausfrau* to invite her neighbors to a round of afternoon beer. The ladies took the beverage with pieces of bread dunked into it—perhaps a forerunner of the modern coffee-klatsch?

This was the epoch when two influences of tremendous impact on the fate of German brewing began to emerge: feudalism and Christianity. Feudalism established controls from above that changed brewing in Germany from a household activity of the common folk into a privileged commercial activity of a favored few, practiced first mostly by monks and nuns and then, since the twelfth century, more and more by secular court breweries and mercantile enterprises. The other influence, Christianity, brought with it the emergence of monasteries not only as beneficiaries of the privileges doled out by the secular lords, but also as centers of education and learning where brewing knowledge could accumulate, standards of quality could improve, and the craft of brewing could evolve, for the first time in Europe, into a true profession.

Enter the Feudal Beer Drinker

Feudalism began to replace the loose social organization of the Germanic tribes as their ancient customs and practices became codified into coherent bodies of law. Ironically, these new laws were written in Latin, the language of the just-ousted oppressor.

The Goths and Burgundians both made new laws in 506. The Franks compiled theirs between 508 and 511. The Alemans got theirs in 719, the Bavarians in 743. These laws granted every household the right to brew beer. They also specified the tributes each had to render as a tax unto the authorities: a certain amount of wood, meat, hemp, grain, honey, wool—and beer.

Under feudalism, money was scarce. Some historians argue that the lack of coinage was one of the main reasons why feudalism took hold in the first place. The Roman system of central administration and taxation had disappeared, as had the benefits that came with it: educational institutions, road and bridge maintenance, trade, a uniform currency. With the Romans gone, most wealth-creating activities ceased, the economy became based on barter as Europe entered the Dark Ages, and for several centuries there was a great and universal decline in population. The principal values in the economy were labor and produce—and each kingdom needed to turn the former, of the which the people had plenty, into the latter, of which the king took plenty. The impetus that made the system work was the people's need for security and protection and the king's ability to grant it.

Effective power in the Dark Ages resided in local dukes, appointed by the king and pledged to him by a personal oath of fealty. These vassals were charged with raising armies for defense and public safety and with carrying out administrative and judicial duties. In exchange the local lords received land, which they in turn subdivided into smaller holdings run by subvassals and worked by serfs. The vassals owed their immediate overlords obedience, war service, and a prescribed number of soldiers, usually recruited from the ranks of the serfs.

The bold and strong eventually rose to become noble knights, and the weak sank to become toiling peasants. In time, social positions became hereditary and the system evolved into pure feudalism, a static, moneyless form of organization, in which the folks at the bottom traded their labor and their freedom for security and protection provided by those at the top.

Charlemagne Makes Beer Official

Such was the system that Charlemagne found when he started his reign in 768. With few means of transportation and communication, an emperor rarely stayed put for long in the capital, which was Aachen (or Aix-la-Chapelle), about 40 miles west of Cologne. Rulers looked after the realm and local matters by traveling from one castle or crown estate to the next. Without much money in circulation, taxes were in the form of the fruits of the land. The emperor traveled to his revenues in order to consume them on location, because they could not travel to him in the form of coins for his treasury.

Charlemagne's empire was organized into great estates, each with a master's house, church, grain mill, forge, bakery, stables, barns, work-shops, peasants' cottages, and, of course, a brewery.

Charlemagne was a great supporter of the brewing craft and insisted that there be a brewery in each of his estates. For his vassals, he wrote an elaborate set of economic ordinances, entitled *Capitulare Caroli*

Emperor Charlemagne, friend of brewers and ruler of Europe, juggling his scepter and his cathedral, a symbolic balancing act between the secular and the sacred powers of his time.

Magni de Villis (The Main Points about Running Charlemagne's Estates), in which he gave rather detailed instructions about almost any aspect of management, including that of the brewery. Whenever he showed up, paragraph 61 kicked in: "We wish that the intendants on duty bring before Our Person samples of beer. We also wish that they bring along their brewmaster so that they can brew for Us good beer in our presence." In paragraph 34, he instructed brewers about hygiene: "The administrators have to make sure that workers who use their hands in the preparation of beer, keep themselves especially clean." He also insisted on annual reports (paragraph 62): "We also wish that our intendants compose an annual inventory ledger at Christmas time. We also want a list of the beers they brew so that we know which quantities of the different products are available" (Hellex 1981).

From this marble throne in the august setting of the Imperial Cathedral of Aachen, Charlemagne managed the affairs of Europe and regulated the quality of beer.

In these ordinances lie the seeds of institutional commercial brewing in central Europe, an activity in which the monasteries were soon to become the most successful players.

If You Got the *Gruit,* You Got the Beer

In the feudal system of land control with a clear division of rights and obligations between lords, vassals, and serfs, all land not specifically granted to a vassal belonged to the crown. And the crown land held a most important resource for the *hausfrau* brewster of the age: Remember, we are still in the prehops era. We know that hop gardens were cultivated in the Hallertau region of Germany as early as the 730s, but for centuries to come beer generally continued to be spiced mostly with *gruit* (old German for "wild herbs") such as yarrow, bog myrtle, or juniper. Thus the quality of the beer you could make depended on your access to suitable herbs, and these grew mostly on uncultivated crown lands. Though everybody was allowed to brew, not everybody was allowed to pick *gruit*. This gave the crown almost accidental control over the quality of the beer in the land. Initially, the crown reserved the *gruit* privilege only for its own estates, although it later granted it to churches and monasteries as well. Eventually, the term *gruit* came to mean not only the herbs brewers used to flavor the beer but also the taxes they had to pay for their brewing privilege.

To Preach and to Brew . . .

At the time of Charlemagne, monasteries were a recent innovation. Outside Italy, the first people to be Christianized were the Irish and the Britons, early in the fifth century. Imbued with missionary zeal, the new converts set out to save continental pagans from damnation. By the beginning of the sixth century, Irish missionaries had started to penetrate the heathen Teutonic forests in search of souls. They founded small monasteries from which they spread the gospel.

A particularly successful missionary was the Irish saint Columban, who, with his band of followers, planted the seeds of the new creed in parts of present-day France, Austria, Germany, and Switzerland. At Saint Gall, in Switzerland, a disciple of his founded the famous monastery that was to become by far the largest brewery of the Dark Ages, which we will look at more closely in chapter 4.

Another famous missionary-brewer was the Franconian monk Corbinian, who, in 724, built a simple chapel on Weihenstephan Mountain, north of Munich. He must have picked a great spot, for the little religious outpost grew into a Benedictine abbey, which, in 1040, obtained from Bishop Engilbert of Freising official brewing privileges and the right to sell its beer for profit. Today the brewery at Weihenstephan is owned by the State of Bavaria and is the oldest continuously operated brewery in the world.

Like all Germanic households, the good brethren of the early Middle Ages grew their own grain and made their own brew. They soon discovered that beer, if made strong enough and from the best grains, was not only thirst quenching but also very nourishing, a veritable "liquid bread." This was important to the monks because of their penchant for periodic fasting, during which no solid food was permitted to pass their lips. Liquids, however, did not break the fast, at least according to ecclesiastic doctrine, which was made up by the church fathers in Rome. The Holy See, of course, knew little about German beer.

Nunneries, too, became centers of institutional brewing. After all, their inhabitants would have become secular beer-making *hausfrauen* had they not chosen the nun's habit.

Naturally, the monks and nuns made more beer than they needed just for their own consumption. As part of their charitable works, they liberally shared both their bread and their beer with the poor and with any traveler or pilgrim who might ask for shelter. Soon, monastery beer gained quite a reputation for quality. As the demand increased, so did the size of the monastic breweries, and some brothers and sisters began to specialize in brewery work.

The Discovery of Hops

Being well-educated people, the friars and nuns took a scientific approach to brewing. They experimented with new techniques and ingredients and created systematic records of the results. In the process, they discovered the virtues of hops as a bittering and preserving agent—though nobody is quite sure exactly when—and probably developed the first beers of consistently high quality. We know that, already in the eighth century, the monastery of Weihenstephan was surrounded by hop gardens, and it is doubtful that the friars cultivated the vine merely for aesthetic reasons.

In a book entitled *Physica Sacra* (Sacred World), we can find the first written description of the preserving and healthful effects of hops in beer. The book's author is Hildegard von Bingen (1098–1179), a Benedictine abbess, brewnun, physician, natural scientist, and advisor to Emperor Frederick I (Barbarossa). Hildegard drank beer regularly and lived to be eighty-one years old, an incredible age for that time. It is not surprising that some people like to see a causal connection between her longevity and her dedication to beer.

Only the female flowers of hops are of any use in beer making. Scientists speculate that it is the estrogen in the hops, not the beer's caloric content, that accounts for the proverbial beer belly in many male beer drinkers.

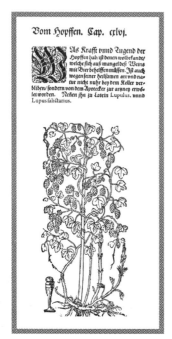

Vom Hopffen. Cap. crlvj.

Als Krafft vnnd Lugend der Hopffen hab/ ist denen wolbekandt/ welche sich auß mangel deß Weins mit Bier behelffen müssen. Ist auch wegen seiner heilsamen art vnd natur nicht nuhr bey dem Keller ver-bliben/ sondern von dem Apotecker zur arpney erwö-let worden. Nennen ihn zu Latein Lupulus. vnnd Lupus salictarius.

Depiction of hops in an old German book on herbs.

Beer Privilege—
A Tool of Governance

Upon his death in 814, Charlemagne left to his heirs a vast empire. By 962 the Germanic tribes in the eastern portion of that land had become firmly united in the first empire officially called "German." At its head was the Saxon Otto I (912–973, also known as Otto the Great). Realizing that the parishes, monasteries, and nunneries represented the only network of public institutions in his realm, he firmly allied himself with the church. Because central government was weak in the feudal system, the church and its bishops took over many governmental functions. Bishops doubled as judges, they organized public works, and, if need be, even buckled on their swords and rode into battle to protect their flocks against foreign invaders or local robber bands.

From kings to serfs, the inhabitants of the feudal world eventually grew to fear the material and spiritual weapons of the church. Otto strengthened the church's position by granting it feudal lay rights and privileges, including the *gruit* right. Soon, the monastic brewers of the early Middle Ages began to enjoy connections in high places. We know that in 947, for instance, Otto I himself conferred the *gruit* right upon the church of Liége (in present-day Belgium). Superior ecclesiastics became themselves grantors of the *gruit* right to their subordinates, as did the Bishop of Metz (in present-day France), when he conferred the *gruit* right onto the nearby monastery of Saint Trond, and the Bishop of Cologne, when he gave it to the church of Neuß (near the present-day altbier home of Düsseldorf).

Beer for Commerce and Salvation

Trade in the Dark Ages was mostly carried out by itinerant peddlers who visited settlements on foot or with pack animals. But they had much to contend with: horrible roads, inclement weather, thievish landlords, piracy, brigands. The monasteries were often the safest refuge for a weary traveler. With Christian fervor on the upswing, pilgrimages, too, became very popular, with Rome and Jerusalem claiming the top of the charts for holy destinations. The hooded fishermen of souls, with hostels and breweries already in place along the old Roman roads, went into the hospitality business with gusto.

Shielded by feudal rights and privileges and confronted with an ever increasing demand for their monasteries' brews, many an abbot eventually succumbed to the commercial temptation and started to sell beer for profit. Cloister inns and pubs began to do a roaring business. Every monastery brewed a different beer and tried to corner the market. The spiritual comrade in the Good Lord's Army soon became the commercial competitor in the beverage business.

Economically, monastic breweries were much like secular businesses but with several competitive advantages: cheap or free raw materials, cheap or free labor, and exemption from all taxes. Monastery beer was good and it was cheap; no wonder that some of these breweries became truly gigantic. The cloister inn at Nürnberg, it is chronicled, eventually made as much as 4,500 buckets (about 2,500 barrels) of beer per year! Another in Bavaria served close to ten thousand guests a year.

The tenth and eleventh centuries were the heyday of monastic brewing in Germany. In a country of perhaps 9 or 10 million inhabitants, there were some five hundred monastery breweries (three hundred in Bavaria alone) producing beer in unsurpassed quantity and quality. And all the beer was ale.

The Monks Had Fun, but the Lords Were Jealous

The commercialization of the monastic brew not only led to its high quality but also to its eventual downfall. Ultimately, the monasteries became victims of the envy and opposition that their successes had bred. The riches garnered from the brewing trade enabled the cloistered community to have a comfortable, secular, and, on occasion, even decadent lifestyle. This became a source of concern to those among the friars who took their vows of poverty, chastity, abstinence, and obedience seriously. It also aroused the envy of the secular lords who, after all, had granted the monks and nuns exclusive brewrights in the first place.

The initial opposition against the secular lifestyle practiced by some of the friars started in the Benedictine Abbey of Cluny in Burgundy, founded in 910. It spawned a movement that quickly spread to almost fifteen hundred affiliated houses all over the realm. The Carthusians at Chartreuse, in the French Alps, started a second monastic revival movement in 1084. The Cistercians at Cîteaux, near Dijon, started a third one in 1098. By the twelfth century a new, purist, antisecular fervor had taken hold in central Europe and led to a gradual redirection of all facets of monastic life. Once again, piety, poverty, and pastoral duties were in, and the secular and profane arts of brewing, commerce, and frolicking were out.

On the political side, too, it seems that the church had overplayed its hand. The struggle between church and state intensified once it became apparent that cloister breweries and pubs, founded under the protection of the secular lords, had generated great riches. Christian philosophers such as Augustine (354–430) had provided the doctrinal underpinnings for the church's claim of preeminence over the state. The church owned about one-third of the land of the realm, and the pope crowned the emperor. Locally, the bishops were not just the spiritual but also the effective civil authorities in the empire. They raised most of the emperor's revenues.

To no one's surprise, the emperor finally insisted on his right to investiture, that is, of appointing his own vassals to the all-important posts of bishop. He could not possibly allow these great officers to be selected by the pope, which would turn the Holy Roman Empire into a hollow shell and the emperor into a mere puppet of an extraterritorial power. The showdown over investiture came in 1077, between Pope Gregory VII and Emperor Henry IV, when Gregory finally played his trump card: He excommunicated Henry. If the Holy See couldn't bask in the temporal glory of earthly might and wealth, the emperor would not be permitted to bask in the eternal glory of heavenly salvation in the Hereafter.

Henry had no choice but to make a pilgrimage to Italy and beg for forgiveness. The two men met at the castle of Canossa near Parma in northern Italy. With Henry on his knees, Gregory reversed the

Gregory VII reformed the calendar (we still use the Gregorian calendar today!), but lost his power poker with the German Emperor Henry IV and died in exile. With a weakened church, many monks and nuns lost their brew privileges.

excommunication in exchange for Henry's abandonment of all claims to investiture. The temporal power of the Holy See—and with it the brew power of the Benedictine monks and nuns—had reached its zenith. The pope had won, so it seemed, and henceforth power and wealth in Germany were to be his to skim. But Henry was back in Italy only seven years later, this time not on his knees but with an army. He captured Rome, forced Gregory into exile, and appointed a new pope. He who laughs last . . .

Let's Have Ourselves a Nice Little *Hofbräuhaus*

The waning of the pope's power that followed Henry's victory had a profound influence on a society run by the church. Where there is a power vacuum, somebody is bound to fill it. The feudal lords, once the benevolent supporters of monastic brewing rights, now became increasingly eager to cash in for themselves on the riches that could be gained from the brew industry. They started to create their own court brew houses (*Hofbräuhäuser)* with exclusive privileges enforced by the sanctions of the law, over which, of course, they had total control. As a result, many monasteries lost the right to brew commercially, though some retained permission to continue to brew for their own consumption.

Hot Days and Cheap Wine

One natural—rather than social or political—cause also contributed to the waning of monastic dominance in the brew industry and to the decline of beer consumption in general. This was a climatic accident that occurred in the first few centuries of the second millennium. The earth underwent a warming trend that allowed grape growing to spread rapidly into ever more northern areas. Especially in southern Germany, good, cheap, and plentiful wine became available and finally rose to be a serious competitor of the once-dominant drink made from grain. Interestingly, as the monasteries started to lose their beer privileges, they quickly capitalized on the new wave and, once again, became the leaders both professionally and commercially in the emerging wine industry and in the production of wine-based distilled spirits and liqueurs.

chapter 4

Saint Gall: Megabrewery of the Dark Ages

■ ■ ■ ■ ■ ■ ■ ■ ■ ■ ■ ■ ■ ■ ■ ■ ■ ■ ■

After the demise of Rome, it fell upon Christian monks to hold the Western world together. Sheltered behind their monastery walls, reflecting on man's soul, virtue, and destiny, the friars created little paradises— refuges in the wilderness where they copied old books, wrote new ones, conducted almost the only schools, and generally preserved culture and learning during the five centuries of economic and cultural stagnation that we call the Dark Ages.

Like the feudal manors around them, medieval monasteries were virtually self-sufficient. They grew their own grain, raised their own meat, baked their own bread, brewed their own beer.

The earliest monasteries in Germany—a few cloister cells grouped around a wooden chapel—typically had their humble beginnings in small missionary outposts often built by Irish monks. Many of these posts were placed strategically along well-traveled routes such as that around Lake Constance, which served as the pilgrims' gateway to the Alpine passes into Lombardy and the city of Rome beyond.

At present-day Bregenz, in Austria, the Irish monk Saint Columban founded a monastery as early as 580. Saint Columban's disciple, Saint Gall, moved farther into the interior and established a hermitage in Switzerland around 590 at a place now named after him, Sankt Gallen. Little did Saint Gall know that his pious little mountain retreat was destined to become the biggest and most raucous brewery and hostelry of all the Middle Ages!

Initially created by men with the impulse to escape the world, monastery life was harsh and simple. Saint Columban had prescribed six lashes for a monk who forgot to say amen or sang out of tune, ten for a monk who notched a table with his knife. He had decreed that meals should be simple and never large. Food and drink should sustain life, not harm it. Drunkenness was forbidden, and the monk who spilled beer had to stand upright and still for an entire night.

But as the flow of pilgrims and other traveling folk increased on the highways and byways of the empire, so did the monasteries' operations. The food, drink, and shelter the monks once shared out of charity with anyone who appeared soon became a commodity offered to the dusty travelers for profit. Not surprisingly, the observance of ascetic rules began to take a backseat to the chores of providing for the itinerant customers. After a day of hard work in the monasteries' fields, kitchens, and breweries, many a monk naturally found more solace in the merry company of his guests than in the austere cloister regimen prescribed by that seemingly un-Irish Irishman Saint Columban.

By the 720s the cloister of Saint Gall had become a full-blown monastery. By around 800 it had become an imperial abbey whose light of spiritual and material culture shone into all of southern Germany. By the 820s its installations included a church, a cloister, a library, a school, a hospital, a pilgrims' hostel, dining halls, the monks' sleeping quarters, dormitories for workers and tradesmen, guest houses for visitors of lofty rank, elaborate gardens and lawns, workshops, bath houses, latrines, a water-powered mill, and *three* breweries.

By 854, Emperor Louis the German abolished the spartan dietary rules crafted by the early cloistered missionaries. Life in the abbey was good, as

we know from Abbot Ekkehard IV, who in 1060 chronicled *Casus Sancti Galli,* the history of Saint Gall. From him we learn that each monk was entitled to seven meals a day with all the bread he could eat. Evenings were reserved for the round table, at which the monks indulged in happy conversation over tankards of brew. Each monk was allotted five *Maß* of beer a day. The term *Maß* is still used in Bavaria today to denote a liter mug. In those days, a *Maß* was any measure between one and two liters. A single monk at Saint Gall, therefore, might have drained as much as one standard U.S. keg of beer a week!

Each of the three breweries at Saint Gall was dedicated to a particular beer style. The first brewery was used exclusively for strong beer, called *celia*. Usually brewed from barley, sometimes from wheat or, frequently, from both, *celia* was reserved for the abbot and his inner circle as well as for distinguished guests. Rarely did the ordinary monks get to taste it.

The second brewery produced regular *cervisa,* a beer of milky-sour taste usually made from oats and flavored with herbs and sometimes with honey *(cervisa mellita).* It was the everyday beer of the monks and pilgrims and was consumed almost incessantly throughout the day.

The third brewery produced *conventus,* a thin beer made of the final runnings from the stronger beers and mixed with fresh extract from malted oats. It was brewed specifically for the abbey's workers and for beggars.

Saint Gall represented the first truly large-scale brewing operation in Europe. Its three breweries were spread out over forty buildings. They yielded about 10 to 12 hectoliters (8 to 10 barrels) of beer a day. In 895, it took more than one hundred monks, about two hundred serfs, and an even larger number of pupils from the monastery's school to tend to the oat and barley fields and to run the breweries. Eventually the monastery's hunger for grain exceeded its own capacity to grow it, and every inhabitant of the vicinity was forced to render unto the friars of Saint Gall one-tenth of his own grain harvest as a tax.

In the granary, as Ekkehard wrote, "the brewing grain was stored and prepared for beer" (Lohberg n.d.). There the monks threshed the reaped grain, then moistened it until it sprouted. It was dried in a separate room in a kiln that shared its heat source with the "second class" brew kettle that was used to make the monks' and pilgrims' *cervisa*. The kiln was big enough to hold the equivalent of about 1,400 gallons, or about 45 barrels—about the size of a small grain silo on a modern dairy farm. Once fully malted, the grain was coarsely crushed in two huge water-powered mortars.

Each brew kettle served as both mash tun and cooker. Unlike most brew kettles of the time, which were heated by hot stones dropped into the mash or by the infusion of hot water, the Saint Gall brew kettles were direct-fired. They were mounted over round furnaces whose walls were made from a mesh of willow reed filled with clay. Each furnace was large enough for a monk to stand up in to patch the clay walls. A flue at the top of the furnace directed the smoke away, either into the open air or into the kiln.

The monks separated the wort from the grain by ladling it out of the kettle with wooden buckets and filtering it through pressed straw into flat wooden tubs made of hollowed tree trunks and located in cooling rooms that were adjacent to the brew houses.

Fermentation occurred in separate tanks placed between the cooling vats. Although yeast and its role in fermentation was unknown at the time, the Saint Gall monks had learned that adding a bit of already-fermenting beer from a neighboring fermenter (rich with active yeast) to a fresh batch or pouring fresh wort over the (yeast) sediment left behind by a previous batch would jump-start fermentation. The monks also learned that mixing the residue from the fermented beer with bread dough in the nearby bake house would make the bread rise faster.

Initially there were no lagering cellars at Saint Gall. There was no need for them. The beers were so popular that they were drunk as soon as they were fully fermented. Only in the twelfth century, when climatic and social changes in Europe lead to a decline in the consumption of monastery beers, did the friars of Saint Gall add a lagering cellar to their operation.

Saint Gall, in all its splendor and opulence, epitomized the greatness of medieval monastic brewing. The beer was, by all accounts, of good and consistent quality, and it was plentiful—an achievement that had been almost five centuries in the making. When circumstances gradually forced the monasteries out of the beer business, it took the medieval merchant-burghers centuries before they were able to connect with the tradition of quality beers that the friars left behind at the close of the Dark Ages.

chapter 5

The Struggle
for Purity—But
Where's the Yeast?

■ ■

Medieval brewster with her tools of the trade.

By the twelfth century, feudal aristocrats, especially in southern Germany, began to take over the brew business from the monasteries and convents. A lord would build his own *Hofbräuhaus* and, if he was charitably inclined, issue a license to a secular private brewery—for a hefty fee, of course, but not always with desirable results. As it turned out, the brewing privileges of the monks and nuns were much more easily transferred than their brewing expertise, and beer quality usually declined.

In northern Germany the story was slightly different. There, forward-looking mercantile entrepreneurs rather than feudal nobles challenged the church for its brew monopoly. The enterprising free burghers usually were fast studies. Eventually they triumphed over the men of the cloth and surpassed them in the quality of the beers they produced.

The Dark Ages Turn Light and the Beer Turns Sour

Most of the brews that were in vogue in the High Middle Ages in southern Germany had very little resemblance to the beers we know today. Water may have been the only ingredient we would recognize with certainty. Brewers used barley, wheat, rye, and oats, even millet, peas, beans, or any other starch-containing kernels in their mash tuns, as long as they could be malted or converted into sugars. Though hops had been known as a flavoring for beer since the eighth or ninth century, any number of herbs, such as caraway or juniper, even salt, pith, soot, chalk, or hard-boiled eggs were used to "improve" the flavor of beer or to cover up off-flavors.

This is how the Nürnberg constabulary dealt with uncrupulous brewers. Their bad beer was hauled to a bridge across the Pegnitz River, from where it was unceremoniously dumped into the rushing waters below.

Regulation to the Rescue

As beer quality fell, so did beer consumption. This called for intervention, if need be at the highest level, lest profits for the noble coffers should suffer. It should come as no surprise then that the noble rulers of the day as well as the civil authorities in the cities suddenly developed a keen interest in preserving the public health—or so they claimed—by regulating the quality of beer.

Emperor Frederick I himself was the author of the first known secular beer regulation in Germany. It dates from 1156 and was part of the first city code of law, the *Justitia Civitatis Augustensis,* that Frederick gave to the city of Augsburg. The emperor decreed that "a brewer who makes bad beer or pours an unjust measure shall be punished; his beer shall be destroyed or distributed at no charge among the poor" (Hellex 1981). The punishment for a violation was five guilders. After the third offense, the perpetrator lost his brewing license.

To control the quality (and revenues) of the local suds, the cities started to issue strict and often silly regulations. The tyranny of bureaucracy in many instances replaced the tyranny of aristocracy.

In 1293 the city council of Nürnberg tried to improve the beer brewed within its walls by issuing a straightforward ordinance in which it insisted that only barley be used to brew beer. Other beer ordinances, however, were not so simple or rational. We know of an early, pesky, lengthy, and meddlesome ordinance that dates from 1351. Issued by the magistrate of the city of Erfurt in Thuringia, it states:

A calibrated tankard must always be filled to the mark. The beer in it shall cost 4½ pfennigs and 8 groschen. No burgher or councilor may brew more than two beers per year, nor may he make half a brew, nor may he mill less or more than three boxes of malt to brew with. Only on Wednesday evening, and not before the beer bell is rung, may he start a fire under the tun and start brewing. But nobody may brew who does not possess containers, tuns, kilns and casks. The beer must be an entire brew. The amount to be brewed must be announced on Walpurgis Day [February 25], and the precise amount announced must then be brewed. Nobody may brew with straw and twigs for fire.

Anybody who breaks an innkeeper's beer mug or runs away without paying, will pay a 10-groschen penalty or must leave town. Anybody who buys hops may not touch the measuring jar until the vendor has filled it and has removed his hand from it. [In those days, brewers bought hops by volume, not by weight!] In the countryside, nobody may sell beer from another region nor may he brew without the knowledge of the town. Any burgher caught brewing in the countryside will no longer be considered a burgher of the town. (Hellex 1981)

Here we find an early version of *Bierzwang* (literally "beer coercion"), the parochial practice of the local authorities permitting only those beers to be served within their walls and in the surrounding countryside that were brewed (and taxed) within their own jurisdiction. The *Bierzwang* remained common in many parts of Germany until 1803, when, under the influence of the Napoleonic conquest of central Europe, *Bierfreiheit* (beer freedom) was finally established as a matter of law in much of Germany.

In 1250 the good citizens of Regensburg, the town where the Romans had already brewed beer some one thousand years earlier, received their brew privileges from Emperor Frederick II. As business thrived, the brewers found it difficult to resist the temptation to raise their profits by lowering their standards. After a disastrous harvest in 1433 and the resulting grain shortage, the local beer became so scarce that the city fathers permitted the importation of brews from as far away as Hamburg and Dortmund. By 1447 the Regensburgers finally had enough of substandard local brew. They appointed their city doctor, Konrad Megenwart, as the official beer inspector and six years later forbade brewers within their city walls to use "seeds, spice, or rushes" as flavorings (Hellex 1981). To ensure that the citizens would get their money's worth, the city fathers also outlawed the brewing and selling of thin beers made from the final runnings of the mash.

In Munich, too, regulating brewers and their craft was of apparent and perpetual concern to the city fathers of the day—and a clear indication that not all was well with the Bavarians' national beverage. In 1363, to guarantee quality, the twelve-member city council itself assumed the duty of overseeing all beer production. By 1372 there were only twenty-one brewers left in Munich, not even two for every councilor, and the demand of the people for beer kept these brewers so busy that their brew was consumed almost as soon as it was fermented. In 1420 the council tried to decree from above what the market would not do on its own. It insisted that all beers must be aged for at least eight days before they could be sold.

In 1450 the number of brewers had risen to only thirty, and the Bavarian ruler, Duke Stephan II, tried to redress the beer shortage by issuing an appeal to his subjects. He implored them to brew more at home so that beer would not be so terribly scarce all the time. It was to take another couple of centuries before the brewers of southern Germany finally caught up with their northern German brethren. In the fifteenth century, however, brewing clearly was not an attractive profession in Munich, the city that was destined to become the beer capital of the world.

Prohibition, the Ultimate Regulatory Weapon

In areas with an emerging wine industry, the answer to declining beer quality was often sought in outlawing beer making altogether. Such was the case in the Franconian city of Würzburg, where the magistrate in 1434, after due consultation with the duke and the bishop, forbade brewing "for ever" (Gerlach et al. 1984). Only three years later, however, the climate of central Europe, which had undergone a warming trend for a few centuries, experienced a sudden reversal. Harsh and long periods of frost decimated almost all the vineyards in southern Germany. Wine had to be imported from south of the Alps, and the price jumped accordingly. Consequently, beer, which had been out of favor with the populace, made a quick comeback.

The authorities, however, with the timeless arrogance of the mighty, stubbornly clung to their prohibition, ignoring both the popular will and the clandestine brewing that it spawned. But greed, as always, got the better of them, and they decided to profit themselves from what they had so miserably tried to suppress. In 1642, Johann Philipp von Schönborn, the Würzburg duke and bishop himself, started his very own *Hofbräuhaus*. Thus, in Würzburg, "for ever" lasted exactly 208 years.

The climatic reversal of 1437 turned out to be long-lasting. It brought about a permanent shift in market forces and gave a much-needed boost to the secular brew industry in southern Germany—and in its wake spawned even more regulation.

Let's Have Purity

In 1447 the Munich city council issued an ordinance demanding that all brewers use only barley, hops, and water for their beers. This was the forerunner of what was to become, half a century later, the famous all-Bavarian beer purity law, the *Reinheitsgebot*. By 1487 the Bavarian Duke Albrecht IV forced all brewers in the city of Munich to take a public oath of faithful allegiance to the 1447 ordinance. Furthermore, the duke introduced beer price controls: In winter, a *Maß* (approximately one liter) would cost one silver pfennig, in summer, two. This price difference was to compensate brewers for the extra grain and long storage (lagering) required for stronger summer beers. One of Albrecht's successors, Duke Georg the Rich, in 1493 extended the 1447 ordinance to the duchy of Landshut in central Bavaria. Clearly, a regulatory cleanup was afoot in Bavaria.

The *Reinheitsgebot* was issued on April 23, 1516. Initially applying only to feudal Bavaria but later to all of Germany, it gave government the tools to regulate the ingredients, brewing processes, and quality of beer sold to the public. It was drafted by the Bavarian corulers Duke

Wie das Pier summer vñ winter auf dem
Land sol gescheuckt vnd praüen werden

Item wir ordnen/setzen/vnnd wöllen/ mit Rathe vnnser
Lanndtschafft/ das füran allennthalben in dem Fürsten-
thůmb Bayrn/auff dem lande/ auch in vnsern Stetten vñ
Märckthen/da deßhalb hieuor kain sonndere ordnung ist/
von Michaelis biß auff Georij/ ain maß oder kopffpiers
über ainen pfenning Müncher werung/ vñ von sant Jor-
gen tag/biß auff Michaelis/ die maß über zwen pfenning
derselben werung/ vnd derenden der kopff ist/ über drey
haller/bey nachgesetzter Pene/nicht gegeben noch außge-
schenckht sol werden. Wo auch ainer nit Mertzn/ sonder
annder Pier prawen/oder sonst haben würde/sol Er d och
das/kains wegs höher/dann die maß vmb ainen pfenning
schencken/vnd verkauffen. Wir wöllen auch sonderlichen/
das füran allenthalben in vnsern Stetten/Märckthen/vñ
auff dem Lannde/zů kainem Pier/merer stück/ dañ al-
lain Gersten/Hopffen/vñ wasser/genomen vñ gepraucht
sölle werdñ. Welher aber dise vnsere Ordnung wissentlich
überfaren vnnd nit hallten wurde/ dem sol von seiner ge-
richtzöbrigkait/ dasselbig vas Pier/ zůstraff vnnachläß-
lich/ so offt es geschiche/ genommen werden. Jedoch wo
ain Gäuwirt von ainem Pierprewen in vnnsern Stettñ/
Märckten/oder aufm lande/yezůzeitñ ainen Emer piers/
zwen oder drey/kauffen/ vnd wider vnnter den gemayn-
nen Pawrsuolck außschenncken würde/ dem selben allain/
aber sonnst nyemandts/sol dye maß/ oder der kopffpiers/
vmb ainen haller höher dann oben gesetzt ist/ze geben/ vñ
außzeschencken erlaube vnnd vnuerpotñ.

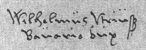

The original text of the *Reinheitsgebot,* the German Beer Purity Law of 1516.

The Verdict of the European Court: Purity Violates Free Trade

Over the centuries the *Reinheitsgebot* gained gradual acceptance for all types of beer in all of Germany. By the time Bismarck forged the Second German Empire in 1871, the *Reinheitsgebot* was in force in many of the kingdoms and principalities that formed the new union. By 1906 it became the official law in all the realm of the Kaiser, by then with the addition of yeast as a basic ingredient and malted wheat as an allowable component in top-fermented beers such as alt, kölsch, and weizen.

Chancellor Otto von Bismarck.

With the formation of the Weimar Republic in 1919, the *Reinheitsgebot* was firmly anchored in the German beer tax law, in part because the then Free State of Bavaria declared that it would not join the new republic unless the *Reinheitsgebot* was enforced in the entire country! The *Reinheitsgebot* survived the upheavals of recent German history, remained on the books during the Third Reich, and is now part of the tax code of the Federal Republic. Even brewers in Norway, Switzerland, and Greece have embraced the canons of the German purity edict.

However, all good things must come to an end. International trade and the global economy have finally—after almost five hundred years—got the better of the famous *Reinheitsgebot.* To the dismay of German brewers, the *Reinheitsgebot,* with its narrow selection of ingredients, was struck down by the European Court in 1987 as a restraint of free trade. The restrictions it contained were held not permissible in the newly integrated European market. After centuries of ensuring beer quality, the *Reinheitsgebot* finally fell victim to the triumph of form over substance. Since the ruling, it has been legal to import beers into Germany that are brewed with adjuncts and treated with chemicals for an artificial head and longer shelf life.

German brewers, however, still adhere fiercely to the *Reinheitsgebot* as a matter of pride and tradition. German beer labels and advertisements still proudly proclaim the purity of the local brew, and many a German imbiber would not think of letting anything but a pure beer pass his or her lips.

Wilhelm IV and Duke Ludwig X and introduced at a meeting of the Assembly of Estates of the Bavarian Realm at Ingolstadt, some 60 miles north of Munich. The 1516 *Reinheitsgebot* stipulated that only barley, hops, and water could be used to make the brew. The existence of yeast had not yet been discovered. The *Reinheitsgebot* is the oldest still-valid food-quality law in Germany.

Whoops! Is That a Lager?

Until the invention of refrigeration in the 1870s, our forebears could not brew what they wanted but only what nature allowed them to. Only gradually did they gain an empirical, trial-and-error understanding of the factors that influence fermentation. They realized that the ambient temperature in the cellar had something to do with the type of beer they got from the wort. They also noticed that there were two types of fermentation.

It would take scientists almost another three hundred years to unravel the mystery of these two fermentations. The crafters of the *Reinheitsgebot* did not know that the key to pure beer is the yeast. Yeasts are airborne single-cell fungi that are literally everywhere in the environment. They like to hide out in dank, dark places. The cobwebs in the grain-dust laden rafters of steamy brew houses made for an ideal yeast habitat. There the yeast spores could idle away their time until luck and a hefty breeze would swish them down into an open fermenter for another sugary meal of sweet wort.

There are two broad families of yeast that make great beers: ale yeasts and lager yeasts, each with their own very specific thermal com-

fort zone. Ale yeasts like a cozy, warm environment somewhere around 59–77 °F (15–25 °C), in which they become most active and produce the best-tasting beer, whereas lager yeasts do their best work when it is a cool 39–48 °F (4–9 °C) or even below.

Ale yeasts lose their appetites at lower temperatures and go to sleep, leaving the field for the lager yeasts. Lager yeasts, on the other hand, can still ferment wort at higher temperatures but then produce off-flavors that tend to be undesirable in beer. Fortunately for the medieval brewers, who had no pure yeast strains to work with, each of the two yeasts, when present in the same brew, becomes dominant in its respective temperature range.

Both ale and lager yeasts are in suspension in the wort while they munch their way through the sugars deep inside the fermenter, but only ale yeasts throw up thick frothy layers of foam at the top of the brew. Ale yeasts, therefore, are also called "top fermenting." Lager yeasts, by comparison, are much less exuberant surface fermenters and are thus often referred to as "bottom fermenting."

After they have done their job of turning wort into beer, both ale and lager yeasts take a nap (go dormant) and generally sink to the bottom.

Because of the temperature-sensitive nature of yeast, the beer the *Reinheitsgebot* originally sought to control was not necessarily a lager. Unbeknownst to the medieval brewer, it was probably a lager during the cold Bavarian winters, but it was most certainly an ale in the summer, when demand was greatest.

A Munich town council record mentioned cold-fermented beer as early as 1420. Again in Munich, in 1551, a city ordinance implied that fermentation was not an accidental process but that it could be managed to produce a definite result. It stated that "barley, good hops, water and yeast [!], if properly mashed and cooled, can also produce a bottom fermenting beer" (Lohberg n.d.). What tantalizing hints at an early awareness of the difference between ales and lagers!

In 1553, summer brewing was outlawed altogether in Bavaria. By then the authorities—always worried about the supply of healthy summer beer—had obviously learned that cold fermentation yielded a purer beer with better keeping qualities than were possessed by those unwittingly brewed and probably bacterially infected top-fermented beers of summer. The official brewing season was, therefore, restricted to between Saint Michael's Day (September 29)

and Saint George's Day (April 23). From spring to fall, brewers had to seek alternative employment.

It is obvious that this kind of brew schedule, decreed from above, favored the production of lagers. In many breweries one simply could not make ales in the cold Bavarian winters.

The importance of the two regulations, the *Reinheitsgebot* and the prohibition against summer brewing, cannot be overstated. These laws caused Bavaria to depart from what had been a common German beer culture. They created a north-south schism between a "new" lager culture and the "old" ale culture. Henceforth, Bavarian brewers would chart their own course, moving firmly in the direction of cold-fermented, malted barley–based lager beers—a style in which, by happenstance and skill, the Bavarians have, some would argue, remained unsurpassed to this day.

When Did the Oktoberfest Really Start?

After the Bavarian summer-brewing prohibition was introduced by the Wittelsbachers, the ruling house of dukes, in 1553, Bavarian brewers started to make Märzen beer, a dark brown lager high in alcohol (as much as 6%) and loaded with hops to ensure its keeping qualities. Mashed-in in March, this beer was stored (lagered) during the hot summer months in caves and cellars packed with ice from the previous winter. Supplies were depleted as summer thirsts grew. At the beginning of the new brewing season in September, any leftover Märzen was consumed liberally to clear the market and the vats and casks for the fresh supplies—an early version of the Oktoberfest?

In Munich, the now famous annual beerfest started almost accidentally, in 1810, as a public celebration of the marriage of Crown Prince Ludwig I of Bavaria to Princess Therese of Sachsen-Hildburghausen. It began innocently enough as a folkfest with horse racing on the *Theresienwiese,* a meadow named after the bride. Because everybody had so much fun the first time around, it was decided to have a repeat of the whole hoopla at each anniversary of the regal nuptials.

Though no liquid libation seems to have been available to the public on that first festive occasion, we know from a report by the German poet Achim von Arnim that, four years later, the festivities already featured an ample array of beer shacks dispensing brew in half-liter tin-lidded steins. Over the years the festival grew until it metamorphosed into the biggest drinking party in the world.

The Märzen Oktoberfest beer too changed from a darkish lager to the amber-colored version we know today. The first of the new Oktoberfest beers was produced by brewmaster Joseph Sedlmayr of the Spaten Brewery in 1871, modeled after a recipe first developed by the Vienna brewmaster Anton Dreher in 1841. Consider that the original Oktoberfest beer would have been a summer-brewed ale had it not been for the summer brew prohibition and the strong Märzen that it spawned! After all, refrigeration had not been invented in the early 1800s.

Today, however, the Märzen, though the traditional Oktoberfest beer, is no longer the biggest seller at the annual Oktoberfest. That honor has passed to the Bavarian helles, also known as helles export, a blonde, malty lager that became the dominant beverage in Bavaria toward the end of the 1920s. It is lighter in body than the Märzen and thus probably lends itself more readily to the ritual ingestion of foamy suds by the liter, to which millions of global revelers each year are expected to conform.

chapter 6

Of Burghers and Guilds and Free Brewers

■ ■ ■ ■ ■ ■ ■ ■ ■ ■ ■ ■ ■ ■ ■ ■ ■ ■ ■ ■

By about the twelfth century we observe the birth of a new class of meritorious city burghers linked in trading associations and employing free, wage-earning tradesmen organized in professional guilds. Feudalism, born of a scarcity of education, money, and commerce, in which land and serfs, as the only sources of wealth, were divided between the learned (the clergy) and the mighty (the nobility), soon became an anachronistic shell for a society whose material basis was shifting from agriculture to industry and commerce. Social control over beer making henceforth was not so much a struggle between the lord and the monk as between the lord and the citizen.

As the monks and nuns were losing their brew privileges, merchants in the cities, perhaps more faithful to their own fortunes than to god and emperor, knew a good thing when they saw one. They latched on to the brewing trade wherever possible and soon found themselves in conflict with church and state alike.

Especially in northern Germany, where, as a general rule, the hold of church and state over society was less smothering, free merchants, not feudal lords, emerged as the greatest competitors to the cloistered brewers. The worldly merchants opened up new markets by setting up far-flung trading organizations, most famous among them the Hanseatic League, for the exchange of all sorts of goods, from spices to salted fish to silk to beer.

The first cracks in the feudal order occurred as early as 924, when King Henry I was forced to build forts and walled towns to protect the eastern flank of his realm against the raids of marauding Magyars. Not getting much help from the noble lords in his fight against the invaders on horseback from the east, the king turned to the ordinary folk and encouraged them to become "burghers" (from the German *Burg,* meaning "castle" or "fort"). With this act Henry not only created a new word but an entirely new class.

As he built defensive bastions in the frontier regions, he ordered their inhabitants to lay in stores of food for emergencies and to train for combat in marching formations and on horseback. On these burghers, the king also conferred the right to brew beer and to sell it within a mile from the fortifications. These military centers soon became the hubs of judicial, commercial, and social activity for the surrounding areas. In these settlements the new class, the middle class, was in time to tear asunder the very foundations of the social order that had evolved in Germany after the collapse of the Roman Empire some five hundred years earlier.

Initially, city brewing, like country brewing, took place only in the home, where it would have stayed had it not been for one problem: In those days, all buildings except for churches, fortifications, and castles were made of wood, and occasionally an entire town would burn down merely because someone had forgotten to tend the fire under the brew kettle or the bake oven. Many city councils, therefore, out of concern for public safety simply forbade home brewing and home baking. They erected communal stone bake-and-brew houses in which every household had to take turns making its daily bread and beer. Such communal bake-and-brew facilities created the physical conditions for the commercialization and the regulation and taxation of city brewing.

As these early city breweries began to hire workers, bakers often doubled as brewers. They already had all the required ingredients on hand. A warm medieval bake house was an ideal habitat for airborne yeast cells to perform their daily work both as leaveners of bread and as fermenters of brew. More often than not, certain yeast strains became dominant in such an environment, as still happens in the rafters and cobwebs of some Belgian lambic houses today, and medieval bakers' beers were usually of consistently good quality.

Thus it was only natural that bakers became the local source of both solid and liquid bread, and many a city authority gladly granted its bakers the exclusive right to make beer. One such fabled baker-brewer even made it into the Grimm brothers' early nineteenth century collection of folk tales (Jakob Grimm, 1785–1863; Wilhelm Grimm, 1786–1859). Sings Rumpelstiltskin, while he dances around the fire in gleeful anticipation of the fruit of his blackmail, "Today I bake, tomorrow I brew, the day after I'll fetch the queen's child."

Patricians of Wealth—The New Force in Brewing

It was inevitable that, sooner or later, many communal brew houses evolved into real businesses with inns attached, where artisans and servants could forget the toil of the day over a mug of ale, and where enterprising burghers could congregate to hatch their profitable deals. Like the monasteries in the countryside, the burgher breweries in the city became thriving businesses, as many a brewpub is today.

In time, the interests of the more successful burghers, the patricians of wealth, would collide with those of the feudal holders of power and privilege, including the beer privilege. The feudal lords, whose only claim to fame was that they had been born into the right families, were not part of the cash economy of the entrepreneurs and were eventually reduced to relying on the generosity of the cities for the financing of their wars and their luxurious lifestyles.

One such successful band of medieval burgher entrepreneurs was the Fugger family of Augsburg. The Fuggers had amassed such wealth

A Nürnberg brewer of 1588. Is this what brewer Rumpelstiltskin looked like?

through banking and trading in real estate, copper, silver, and mercury that by the fifteenth century they were by far the richest family in Europe.

Emperor Maximilian I (1459–1519) relied on immense Fugger loans to finance his foreign wars, and in 1519, when it was time to choose Maximilian's successor, the Fuggers secured the election of their man, Charles V, as emperor by bribing the electors. It was Charles V (1500–1558), ruler of most of Europe, including Austria and Germany as well as Spain and her colonies around the globe, who could claim, as the first monarch

The noble Emperor Maximilian I financed his foreign wars with loans from common merchant burghers, many of whom traded in beer, which begs the question: Who really ran Germany in the late Middle Ages, the folks with the power or the folks with the money?

Imperator Caesar Diuus Maximilianus Pius Felix Augustus

in history, that in his empire "the sun never set," but it was the rising sun of the merchant class that had put him on the throne in the first place.

For such support, of course, the titled rulers had to pay a hefty price. They were forced to grant the cities virtual self-government and an ever increasing share in the government of the realm. In 1521, at the Diet of Worms, Charles conferred upon the city of Augsburg the right to mint its own coins. It is hard to imagine that such favors were not in payment to the Fugger family of Augsburg, to whom he owed so much.

Cities, in effect, became "free." In their charters they received the right to make laws, mint coins, levy taxes, and run their own commercial and political affairs without interference from the nobles. *Stadtluft macht frei* (city air liberates) was the slogan of the burghers, and it enticed many a serf to slip away by night and escape feudal oppression. Serfs were owned, literally, by their feudal masters, who gave them no other reward for their labors but the rations needed for their families' subsistence. Once in the city, a serf became a free person, who could hire himself out in exchange for wages. He could finally take a greater hand in his own destiny.

The burghers made good use of the growing labor pool from the countryside. They organized manufactures, employed serfs as free craftsmen, established trading networks, and built storehouses and retail outlets. Their commercial activities brought ever more wealth and power to the cities until the might of the cities surpassed that of the official feudal system and its agrarian economy.

As no-nonsense merchants, the city burghers plied any trade that offered the promise of profit. And as monks and nuns had demonstrated before, one could get rich on beer, especially on top-quality beer. Thus, the most consequential challenge to the brew monopoly of the medieval church came ultimately not from the nobles but from the rising class of patrician city burghers, especially in northern Germany.

To be sure, there were plenty of arrogant aristocrats and pampered bishops in northern Germany, as there were many enterprising merchant burghers, like the Fugger family, in southern Germany, but as a general rule the northerners pursued their aims of civil and economic freedom more aggressively, sometimes even by force of arms, than did their southern counterparts, and, between the thirteenth and the sixteenth centuries, while beer production and beer quality declined in the south, beer became mostly a northern German affair.

The city burghers and their councils had gained virtual control over the brewing industries within their walls by the end of the twelfth century. Like the nobles before them, city governments often declared that they alone owned the exclusive right to brew. The nobles, hearkening to a world order that was no more, were powerless to stop them.

The Struggle in Cologne

One prominent example of that struggle occurred in Cologne, where, at the height of the feudal era, all power sprang from the archbishop. By the middle of the twelfth century, as most everywhere else in Germany at the time, Cologne's patrician burghers and their wage-earning tradesmen vied with the bishop for power. To the chagrin of the bishop, some burghers had started civil breweries to compete with the monastic monopolies held by the church.

As free-enterprise brewing—and the wealth that came with it—grew in Cologne, two jealous forces mounted their attacks against the prosperous brewers: In an attempt to divide and conquer, the bishop tried to regain control of the industry by restricting the right to brew, sell, and dispense beer to only a few of the city's patricians. The chosen few agreed among themselves to become specialists in either *gruit* or honey beer (hops were not yet in wide use in the Rhineland).

Coat of arms of the city of Cologne.

Those who were left out of the deal mounted their counterattack through the city council, which also wanted to partake in the profits generated by the brewer's craft. By 1212 the council had persuaded Emperor Otto IV to grant the city's civil administration the right to levy taxes on the finished beer. This involuntary donation by the brewers to the public coffers was on top of the standard raw-material taxes they were already

paying on malt—and on top of the excise taxes they were paying on their brew kettles. The three brew taxes—not surprisingly— went up year after year, until the brewery owners of Cologne became the most heavily taxed inhabitants of the city. A fight between the patrician brewery owners on the one hand and the city council and the bishop on the other became inevitable.

In 1238, Archbishop Conrad of Hochstaden succeeded in persuading Otto IV's successor, Emperor Frederick II, to transfer the beer-tax monopoly from the city council back to the sacred authority in Cologne. The city council naturally objected. Both sides called in the Dominican monk Albertus Magnus (later to become archbishop of Cologne himself) to mediate.

He proposed a Solomonic compromise that pleased both the church and the council but not the brewers: The tax revenues from the brewing trade were to remain in place but henceforth would be split fifty-fifty between the coffers of the church and the treasury of the town.

Unintended Consequences of a Cologne Plot

No doubt the free brewers of Cologne needed to be better organized. They did not become officially recognized as a separate occupation until they started their own guild in 1254, though the city council had legitimized forty-nine other crafts guilds about a hundred years earlier. Eager to supply the burgeoning trading network in beer, the breweries banded together to regulate the profession and to ensure the consistent quality, reputation, and profit to be derived from the local beer.

Crest of the brewers' guild of Cologne.

Nobody could practice a trade without being a member of a guild. Guilds became closed shops that set workmanship guidelines, standardized the training of apprentices and journeymen, issued master certificates, regulated advertising and competitive practices, defined membership criteria, specified wages, determined production quantities, looked after members in need, and punished violators of the guilds' rules. Members met at their guild houses to discuss professional, political, and economic issues. The patrician burghers and the tradesmen guilds were the medieval forerunners of our modern management and labor unions.

The immediate target of the Cologne brewers' guild was the bishop. As a relic of the old order, he needed to be knocked off the chessboard first. The opportunity came in 1288, when the rising secular power in the Rhineland was the Duchy of Berg. Its ruler was Duke Adolf V, the protagonist of the plot. The antagonist was the head of the church at the time, the scheming, ambitious archbishop of Cologne, Siegfried of Westerburg.

The burghers of Cologne formed an alliance with Adolf V, who in turn enlisted the help of one flamboyant knight, Duke John I (also known as Jan Primus or Gambrinus), ruler of Brabant and Flanders to the west. Archbishop Siegfried secured the military help of the Duke of Luxembourg and the Duke of Geldern, who were both interested in containing the rising influence of Adolf V.

On June 5, 1288, about six thousand combatants marched on Worringen (outside Cologne) to engage in one of the bloodiest battles of the Middle Ages, which, though not related by the history books, had unintended consequences for the course of German beer making. The Battle of Worringen lasted from dawn until dusk. In the end, the church's forces were routed, and the shepherd of souls, Siegfried of Westerburg, found himself prisoner in Adolf's camp. Fifteen months in a dark, dank dungeon in Adolf's fortress *Burg,* near Wuppertal, turned out to be less than congenial to the archbishop's health, and his family paid a handsome ransom for his release. The Battle of Worringen, however, could not be undone. It broke the secular power of the Cologne bishopric for good and established the supremacy of the civil power in the Rhineland.

With the archbishop out of the picture, the patricians and guilds of Cologne wasted no time in moving into the power vacuum he left behind. Henceforth Cologne was to be ruled by a forty-nine-member chamber that was made up of representatives elected by the guilds and patricians.

To spite his vanquished ecclesiastic foe, Duke Adolf V of Berg decided to create a new city as a competitor to Cologne: On August 14, 1288, he granted a little hamlet two dozen miles farther down the Rhine by the name of Düsseldorf a city charter. Thus began the rivalry between two Rhenish metropolises and two Rhenish ales. Ironically, Düsseldorf and its beers were helped into existence by the anti-clerical burghers of Cologne.

The coat of arms of the city of Düsseldorf. The anchor symbolizes the city's harbor on the Rhine, the lion, the strength of the city's founding father, Adolf V of Berg.

To promote Düsseldorf's growth, "foreign" serfs from outlying areas were enticed to come to the new city on condition that, for a year and a day, they incurred no debts. The serfs of the Duke of Berg, however, were not allowed to emigrate and become free Düsseldorfers. For the next two centuries Düsseldorf's population increased, but the city remained in the shadow of its larger and more important neighbor until the sixteenth century, when it emerged from its deep sleep and gave Cologne a run for its influence—and its beer.

Düsseldorf in 1585.

Gambrinus, the King of Beer

This fanciful image of King Gambrinus, the alleged inventor of beer, dates from 1526 and is now in the Deutsches Brauerei-Museum (German Brew Museum) in Munich.

Almost any chronicler of the history of beer feels compelled to devote a few words to that mythical figure Gambrinus, the alleged king of beer.

This much we know. Gambrinus did live, between about 1250 and 1294, but he did not, as legend would have it, invent beer, nor was his reputation as a superboozer of lasting significance. Then who was this fellow, and what did he do to become the patron of brewers the world over?

His real name was John I, Duke of Brabant and Flanders (now part of Belgium). "John" is "Jan" in Flemish, and "first" is *primus* in Latin. So he was called Jan Primus, which was later mangled—we don't really know how—to Gambrinus. Jan was a great supporter of the brewers' guilds of Leuven and Brussels, and he was well known for partying all night while downing the liquid fruits of his protégés' labors.

Duke Jan was a wild and woolly knight, a legend in his own time, known equally well for exceptional bravery, revelry, and chivalry. He traveled the lands of Brabant, Flanders, and France as swordsman, troubadour, and heartbreaker. His amorous adventures, the story goes, were as countless as the pretty babies and duped husbands he left in his wake.

One such *affaire d'amour,* with the wife of a French knight named Valseneuve, finally was Jan's downfall. The itinerant minnesinger had not reckoned with Valseneuve's priest, who, far from being a model of chastity, had himself a more than casual acquaintance with the bedchamber of the lady of the castle. To the misfortune of our amorous Jan, the spurned and jealous priest got wind of his former lover's transgressions—and told her husband.

The irate Valseneuve, his honor besmirched, did what every self-respecting knight of the age would have done: He challenged Jan Primus to a duel at the next tournament. Jan's *affaire de cœur* had become Valseneuve's *affaire d'honneur.*

Our Don Juan accepted, of course. Before the battle he drank and caroused all night, as was his custom. He thought he had nothing to worry about. The following day, the chronicler tells us, Jan was still fit and nimble-footed. During the duel he kept the noble Frenchman on the defensive, until the latter, perhaps sensing his imminent demise, resorted to a ruse: "What is this?" he yelled. "Does the chivalrous knight need a second man to fight me?" (Ehrenfels-Mehringen 1953). Jan was incredulous, and as he turned around to check who the uninvited—and nonexistent—helper might be, Valseneuve moved in for the kill.

Jan Primus, the flamboyant son of a gun, may have lost that battle and his life, but he won another battle, whose significance for the history of German beer has escaped all the conventional chroniclers: Jan Primus, together with his pal, Duke Adolf V of Berg, won the Battle of Worringen (near Cologne) on June 5, 1288. As a result of that victory, the archbishop of Cologne lost all his secular powers, a rival city named Düsseldorf was founded down the Rhine, and a new ale, the alt, emerged in the Rhineland to rival the kölsch ale of Cologne.

Had it not been for Jan Primus there still would have been beer in the universe, but there might not have been an alt!

This wooden statue of Gambrinus with cask and goblet proves that myth is often more enduring than fact. It was carved by an unknown Franconian artist towards the end of the seventeenth century and belongs now to the Bayerische Brauerbund (Bavarian Brewers Federation) in Munich.

chapter 7

A Private Trading Empire Built on Beer

■ ■ ■ ■ ■ ■ ■ ■ ■ ■ ■ ■ ■ ■ ■ ■ ■ ■ ■

By the thirteenth century many merchants fully understood that the feudal state could no longer adequately protect their interests at home or abroad. Especially in the towns involved in trade with the Baltic lands, civic associations and merchant guilds joined forces to form trading leagues. The merchants of Bremen and Hamburg, for instance, set up a joint representation in Novgorod, in Russia, to deal with the czar.

In London, King Henry II granted German city merchants special licenses and privileges as early as 1157. He even gave them a special residence, a guild hall, later to be called the Steelyard House, on the Thames. In 1194, King Richard I granted the Steelyard merchants from Cologne freedom from all tolls and customs in London and the right to trade at fairs throughout England. These rights were later extended to the other members of the Steelyard. Soon the Steelyard became a walled-in community complete with its own warehouses, weigh house, church, offices, and residential quarters. It spawned affiliated houses in many other English ports.

Political impotence within the Holy Roman Empire of the German Nation as well as difficulties experienced by its seafaring merchants with pirates, feudal regulations against foreign trade, and excessive customs fostered an ever closer union among the leading German trading cities. In 1241, Lübeck and Hamburg, on either side of the

The Hanseatic trade routes converged here at the Holstentor, the city gate of Lübeck.

Danish Peninsula, concluded a treaty of mutual protection, a patrician alliance. In 1266, King Henry III of England gave the Steelyard merchants of Hamburg and Lübeck their own separate charter, making them the most powerful merchant colony in London.

Other German cities soon joined the protective association of Hamburg and Lübeck, and a strong formal alliance, the Hanseatic League, grew up among them, with Lübeck, the center of the Baltic trade, as its hub. The League eventually included some two hundred cities. It fought and won its own wars, as, for instance, in 1368–1369, against the Danish king Waldemar IV, whose countrymen, reminiscent of Viking times, had taken to piracy and helped themselves regularly to "free" beer from the League's freighters. The League signed its own peace treaties with foreign governments. One such was the Treaty of Stralsund (1370), which gave it a virtual trade monopoly in all of Scandinavia. Henceforth, no Danish king could be crowned without the League's formal approval.

The League traded in almost any type of commodity, including wine, oil, grain, leather, cloth, copper, iron, salt, and beer. Thanks to the League, a consumer could buy Polish mustard in England, Turkish

Beer transport in Hamburg.

raisins in Flanders, Italian figs in Norway, and German beer in Russia. By cutting out the feudals, the League had created, in effect, the first European common market, free of tariffs and artificial trade restrictions.

Not just port cities like Bremen, Hamburg, and Lübeck were part of the Hanseatic League. Cities farther inland, such as Einbeck, Brunswick, Breslau, Magdeburg, Dortmund, and Cologne, too, were eager to join the new network and supply the growing trading empire with goods, of which beer became one of the more important export commodities.

Soon wagonloads of export ales would rumble down the dusty northern highways on their way to the harbor storehouses of the Hanseatic merchants. Bremen took the early lead in beer exports, sending casks of German ale as far as Flanders, England, and Scandinavia. The Brunswick mumme, a brown, very hoppy barley ale, was so strong that it remained palatable almost forever and made its way on sailing ships around the globe, even to the hot East Indies.

Horseshoes and Harness Make Beer Trade Possible

The golden age of the beer trade was made possible not only by the ever improving keeping qualities of the northern beers but also by momentous advances in animal traction and harness. Improvements in these areas were first reported in the ninth century but came into wider use only around the thirteenth century. Before that time, a horse was hitched to its dray by traces fastened to a yoke on its withers and anchored by a strap around the breast. The harder the horse pulled, the more the strap choked it. The rigid collar changed all that. It put the strain on the horse's shoulders instead of on its windpipe, thus increasing the animal's leverage almost fivefold. Only then did the transport of heavy casks of beer over rutty roads become possible.

Horses employed in freight hauling were also susceptible to slipping, hoof breakage, and foot injuries. Because of frequent breakdowns in the hay burners, delivery schedules for trading goods were notoriously unreliable. It was not until the arrival of the nailed-on iron horseshoe, which kept the animals sound and surefooted, that trade, especially in semiperishable goods, could be conducted on anything resembling a timetable.

Beer Wars in the Hinterland

Many brewers' guilds had improved the quality of their cities' beer by being intolerant of sloppy brew practices. The flip side of the growing strength of the guilds was the prohibition of outsiders' beers. A guild that had the city council in its pocket could enforce a local monopoly for its own products to the exclusion of beer from neighboring cities. If a brewer from another city ignored the ban, fights would ensue, as happened between Dortmund and its Westphalian neighbors in the early 1300s, and the Saxon towns of Zitta and Görlitz in the 1370s. In such conflicts, armed militiamen often ambushed beer transports and destroyed the casks.

The skirmish over Dortmund beer was particularly nasty. Adolf of Nassau, who was king of Germany between 1292 and 1298, and always short of cash, had sold the brewright to the city of Dortmund one year after his accession to the throne. Soon thereafter, other Westphalian cities, such as Münster, Bielefeld, Hamm, and Minden, also acquired the right to brew beer. In an effort to protect the tax revenues from their local beer production, these upstart brew centers quickly forbade the importation of Dortmunder beer. To make their wishes known, they sent a letter to that effect to the Dortmund city hall.

Unperturbed by the ban, the Dortmunders kept on coming with their casks of "export," whereupon the neighboring cities hired sharpshooters to ambush the beer wagons en route and put musket holes into the wooden casks. In an unprecedented case of beer-war escalation, the Dortmunders, in turn, hired their own mercenaries, whose job it was to exert fitful revenge on the shooters: When caught, the musketeers were unceremoniously drowned in beer.

In 1472, the city fathers of Dortmund handed the thus-defended brewright over to every "full citizen" (read "member of the brewers' guild"). Over the next five centuries the fine burghers of Dortmund made such good use of the privilege that, today, the city has the largest beer production of any city in all of Europe—more than 6 million barrels annually.

How the Bock Got to Bavaria

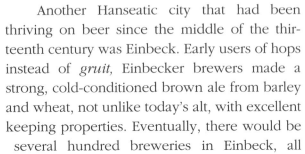

Another Hanseatic city that had been thriving on beer since the middle of the thirteenth century was Einbeck. Early users of hops instead of *gruit,* Einbecker brewers made a strong, cold-conditioned brown ale from barley and wheat, not unlike today's alt, with excellent keeping properties. Eventually, there would be several hundred breweries in Einbeck, all strictly regulated—and taxed—by the city council. Einbeckers shipped their brew by wagon trains to Hamburg, Bremen, and Lübeck, whence it sailed in the holds of Hanseatic ketches to places like Amsterdam to the west and Reval (now Tallinn in Estonia) to the east, and even to Jerusalem, where it may have quenched the thirst of crusading knights.

Perhaps the most important destination of Einbecker beer, at least from hindsight, was Munich. Bavarians who could afford it—especially the nobles—would drink the ale from Einbeck before they would swig the lower-quality local brew.

The Bavarian answer to the competition was twofold. They issued the *Reinheitsgebot* and started to imitate the northern brews locally, though at first to no avail. The imports from the north kept on coming. They remained the most popular drink in Munich, and by 1569 there were still only fifty-three small breweries in the entire city.

The beers from the north were good but expensive and a constant drain on Bavaria's money supply, much to the chagrin of Duke Wilhelm V. He ran his own brew house in Landshut, where, in 1590, he had a new beer brewed, a strong brown to red lager that he hoped would finally recapture the market lost to the northern brewers. A year later he completed a new brew house in Munich on the site of the now famous *Hofbräuhaus*. By 1610, that Munich court brew house made its first deliveries to local innkeepers and private households.

But it was Wilhelm V's successor, Duke Maximilian I, who landed a grand coup that finally spelled an end to the dominance of northern beers in Munich. In 1612 he enticed one Einbecker brewmaster, Elias Pichler, to come to Munich and create an authentic copy of the famous original Einbecker beer. Once there, poor Elias was not allowed to leave town for purpose or pleasure. He had become too valuable a state asset to be allowed to run free. The Bavarian dialect soon mangled the name Einbeck to *ayn pock* and, eventually, to *ein Bock*. The beer itself metamorphosed, under Bavarian influence, from a strong ale into a strong lager, which is what we know as bock beer today.

The popularity of Elias's beer became so great that Maximilian was able to finance most of his military expenditures during the Thirty Years' War out of the revenues from the brown lager made by this transplanted brewmaster. Bavaria was finally on its way to becoming the beer stronghold it is today.

The Cool North, a Hotbed of Brewing

As more and more beer passed through the Hanseatic port city of Bremen, its merchant burghers soon figured that they could make more money by making the beer themselves instead of just buying it from others and trading in it. By the end of the thirteenth century, thanks to the skills of Bremer brewers and to the sheer size of the markets of the Hanseatic League, no beer was more popular and plentiful in Europe than that brewed in Bremen.

The Hamburgers, too, soon entered the international beer business and, during the fourteenth century, started to eclipse their rivals from Bremen. Hamburg emerged as the brewing city of the League, though Bremen continued to be the premier export harbor for beers from Einbeck, Göttingen, and Brunswick. By 1376,

Hamburg recorded 457 burgher-owned breweries, by 1526 there were 531. Together they brewed almost 25 million liters per year (more than 200,000 barrels) and employed almost half the city's wage-earning population. Their most famous brew was *Keutebier,* a hopped, reddish to dark brown wheat beer with an up-front sweetness and a viniferous aftertaste.

One of the more ardent lovers of Hamburg beer was Luther's Reformation cohort and confidant, Philipp Melanchton. Even on his deathbed, in Wittenberg in 1560, Philipp asked for a bowl of beer soup. Knowing it would be his last meal, he specified that it be made with Hamburg suds. How is that for brand loyalty?

The Hannoverians developed their own version of a wheat ale, the Broyhan beer, named after Cord Broyhan, a Hannover native who had left his hometown to apprentice with a Hamburg brewer. There he learned the secrets of Hamburger beer. When he returned home in 1526 he started his own brewery and made his variation on the Hamburg theme, a well-hopped light brown ale mashed from one-third wheat and two-thirds barley.

Soon other entrepreneurs jumped on the Broyhan bandwagon. In 1609 the city council of Hannover regulated the quality and brew techniques of the local Broyhan beer, limited the number of brewer burghers to 317, combined all of them into one guild, and incorporated the guild as a company. The guild brewery still exists today as a stock company and is the oldest commercial enterprise in Hannover.

It was the Thirty Years' War (1618–1648) that sounded the death knell of the Hanseatic League, and with it the glory of northern brewing. After the war's disruptive turmoil, which pitted the Protestant against the Catholic countries of Europe, Germany was devastated. Its cities were plundered, its fields lay fallow, its soil was blood-soaked, its commerce was at a standstill, and the Holy Roman Empire was reduced to a mere shell of its former greatness. Many monasteries and feudal castles lay in ruins, as did their breweries, never to be rebuilt. Germany was split into 370 semi-autonomous states and statelets, all with their own trade restrictions and with borders and customs duties that made trade virtually impossible.

Frau Luther Was a Brewster

If reform of a corrupt and secularized church was the first thing on Martin Luther's mind, beer probably was the second. In the early years of his life he was particularly fond of Einbecker beer, in later years he became more partial to Hamburger beer.

We know that beer sustained him during two important days of his life: his trial and his wedding.

In 1521 Luther had been summoned, during Lent, to appear before the Diet of Worms to defend his antipapal stand. Duke Erich I of Brunswick gave Martin a cask of Einbecker beer to help him through this ordeal. It did the trick, in a way: Luther's defiant performance at the trial earned him excommunication, and the Reformation was underway.

On June 13, 1525, Martin Luther, a former monk, was married to Katharina of Bora, a former nun. For the occasion, Martin received another cask of Einbecker beer, this time from the town of Wittenberg, where he had lived since 1508. However, such valuable liquid gifts soon became quite superfluous, for Luther's new wife had been a trained brewster at the convent of Nimptschen, near the Saxon town of Grimma, where she had received her brewing license. After the marriage, Katharina kept up her brewing skills, and Martin was so fond of her beer that he sent for it whenever he had to be away from home for long periods.

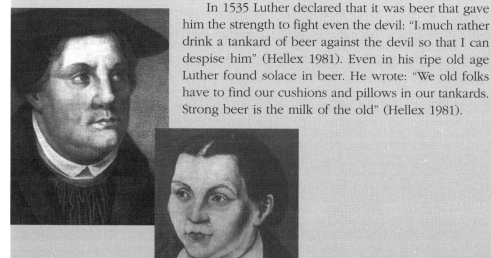

In 1535 Luther declared that it was beer that gave him the strength to fight even the devil: "I much rather drink a tankard of beer against the devil so that I can despise him" (Hellex 1981). Even in his ripe old age Luther found solace in beer. He wrote: "We old folks have to find our cushions and pillows in our tankards. Strong beer is the milk of the old" (Hellex 1981).

Martin Luther, a beer aficionado and former monk, marries Katharina of Bora, a brewster and former nun.

The Hanseatic League formally dissolved in 1669, but its lasting legacy was a change in the economic balance of power in Europe away from the landed feudal nobility to the city-dwelling bourgeoisie. In its wake, the Thirty Years' War left a vacuum waiting to be filled by new social organizations and an openness to new ideas that would bring progress in all facets of life.

chapter 8

Wheat Ales: An Upper Crust Quaff Makes a Flip-Flop

■ ■ ■ ■ ■ ■ ■ ■ ■ ■ ■ ■ ■ ■ ■ ■ ■ ■ ■

The old feudal rulers of the Duchy of Bavaria, the House of Wittelsbach, came to power in 1180. Whatever its political fortunes, as guardian of its subjects' beer it has a lot to answer for. For the first three hundred years of its reign, it tried to keep the brewing of ales and lagers—and the profits that came with it—out of the hands of the monks and the burghers and reserved it for its members and their cronies. Then, for the next one hundred years or so, it almost wiped out ale brewing by passing regulations that favored lager making in general and strengthened the market position of its own court breweries in particular. In the end, though, it reinstated ale making, but only as wheat beer—and then monopolized it completely after it became clear how much money could be made from it.

Today when we think of ales, we picture in our minds a beer that is hearty, full-bodied, satisfying, nourishing, and substantial. When we think of lagers by comparison, we picture a beer that is delicate, subtle, dainty, and gentile. Not so in the Bavaria of the sixteenth century. After the beer purity law of 1516 (the *Reinheitsgebot)* and the summer brew prohibition of 1553, barley-based lagers were brown and smoky, whereas wheat-based ales were "white beers" (weissbier) that were crisp and delicious.

Wheat Beer Is a Useless Drink!

In Bavaria, as in the rest of Germany, any grain was acceptable for beer brewing, until the Wittelsbacher dukes Wilhelm IV and Ludwig X proclaimed that wheat would not make "pure" beer. That assertion must have been a kick in the teeth to the Degenberg clan, a noble family from the village of Schwarzach, near Munich, that had been brewing wheat ales for decades. The Degenbergers considered themselves the sole owners of the privilege to make and sell the brew in Bavaria.

The notable omission by the dukes of wheat as a legitimate raw material for beer in the original *Rein-heitsgebot* is probably no accident but rather a combination of vanity, paternalism, politics, and fiscal avarice. The dukes considered weissbier too gentile a beverage for the vulgar masses, for whom the brown lagers of the time were deemed good enough, especially after the dukes had decreed that they be pure.

Also, there were frequent wheat shortages in medieval Bavaria, and the dukes, well acquainted with their subjects' gustatory habits, feared that the good Bavarians would rather forgo their daily bread than not have their daily brew. Since it was the God-given duty of the feudal lords to look after the welfare of their subjects, they held, in their paternal wisdom, that wheat would best serve the common good if it were consumed in solid rather than liquid form. The dukes considered wheat beer "a useless drink that neither nourishes nor provides strength and power, but only encourages drunkenness" (Lohberg n.d.)—unless, of course, it was destined to slacken a noble thirst! By 1566, fifty years after the *Reinheitsgebot,* wheat-beer making by the ordinary brewer was outlawed altogether.

Wheat Ale Becomes a Political Football

On the political side, the dukes had to respect the inherited monopoly of wheat-beer brewing enjoyed by the House of Degenberg. Blatant revocation of a feudal privilege was unthinkable in an era when the power of the state to make war depended on the willingness of the landed gentry to supply the infantry with serfs. The local lords, who owned the serfs, traded the military services of their subjects for rights and privileges. They usually drove a hard bargain, exacting advantages for themselves in perpetuity.

Although Wilhelm IV confirmed and even extended the Degenbergers' right to brew and sell weissbier, his successor, Duke Albrecht V, however, was not so generous. He tried to make life and business as difficult as possible for the Degenbergers by putting a sales tax on their suds, thus provoking a feud between the two houses, the Wittelsbachers and the Degenbergers, that lasted until 1602. In that auspicious year, happily for the dukes, the line of Degenbergers became extinct, when its last descendant, Baron Hans Sigmund of Degenberg, died without leaving an heir. By the rules of the day, the wheat beer privilege automatically reverted to the house of the Bavarian dukes.

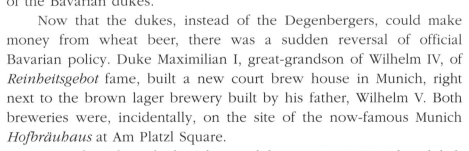

Now that the dukes, instead of the Degenbergers, could make money from wheat beer, there was a sudden reversal of official Bavarian policy. Duke Maximilian I, great-grandson of Wilhelm IV, of *Reinheitsgebot* fame, built a new court brew house in Munich, right next to the brown lager brewery built by his father, Wilhelm V. Both breweries were, incidentally, on the site of the now-famous Munich *Hofbräuhaus* at Am Platzl Square.

Maximilian I brought the Schwarzach brewmaster to Munich and dedicated the new brewery exclusively to weissbier making. Over the years he added more and more wheat beer breweries to his brew conglomerate. He also continued to prevent anybody else from brewing wheat beers and thus granted to the line of Wittelsbachers the only exception to the barley-only provisions of the *Reinheitsgebot*. Do as I say, not as I do!

Not only was wheat beer now permitted to be dispensed to the masses but in fact every innkeeper *had* to pour it, next to the standard brown lager, and purchase it directly from the crown! If an individual refused, he lost his license. This new twist in Bavarian beer policy not only kept the wheat beer flowing in the land but the coffers swelling in the ducal treasury as well.

A Useless Drink Earns Useful Revenues

The weissbier monopoly remained with the Wittelsbachers until well into the nineteenth century, by which time the Bavarian rulers had earned astronomical sums from the sale to the humble masses of the erstwhile upper crust quaff. They even issued a wheat beer quality ordinance, in 1803, in which they specified that the brew should "be bubbly and foamy, contain the bitterness of the hops, leave a cooling and refreshing sensation on the palate, and impart its prickly flavor to its bouquet as well" (Lohberg n.d.).

Thus, in spite of the *Reinheitsgebot,* which put lagers on the map, Bavaria became also the cradle of German wheat ales by decree from above, not by democratic market forces from below, simply because there was money in it for the nobles.

Wheat Beer's Death and Resurrection

Eventually, though, the brown lager of Bavaria improved and made a comeback. By 1808 the ducal brown beer brewery incorporated the adjacent wheat beer brewery into its operations. By the mid-1800s wheat beers had become just a curiosity from the past. In 1872 the Wittelsbachers sold the weissbier privilege to a private brewing company and thus ended two and a half centuries of the ducal wheat beer monopoly. In the decades that followed, wheat beer sales stabilized.

Though the *Reinheitsgebot* has changed in modern times and now allows for malted wheat in certain beers, the weissbier has not. It's still an ale. There is no lager wheat beer in Germany. It would be against the law! All beers called weizen or weissbier must be made with top-fermenting yeast and at least 50% malted wheat. Furthermore, the addition of unmalted wheat—or unmalted anything, for that matter—is *verboten*.

Today, dozens of private breweries turn out wheat ales in all shades of color and alcoholic strength—from clear, blonde, filtered kristallweizen to pale, unfiltered hefeweizen to dark dunkelweizen, to strong weizenbock and even weizendoppelbock. Ales made from wheat in some regions now constitute some 10% of all beer consumption and are available in stores and pubs across the country from Hamburg to Munich and Düsseldorf to Dresden.

Courtesy of Privatbrauerei Hoepfner, Karlsruhe, Germany.

Early "cold machines" (refrigeration units) such as this gave brewers for the first time effective control over fermentation temperature and thus allowed them to make both ales and lagers at will, anywhere, year-round.

chapter 9

Here Come de Yeast . . . and Modern Brewing

▪ ▪ ▪ ▪ ▪ ▪ ▪ ▪ ▪ ▪ ▪ ▪ ▪ ▪ ▪ ▪ ▪ ▪ ▪

Even after the demise of the Hanseatic League and the stagnation of the brew industry in the north, free brewing continued in Germany. In Bavaria, monastery and court breweries were being replaced by commercial ones. Although between the twelfth and sixteenth centuries, much of the top-quality brew consumed in Bavaria had to be imported from northern Germany, by 1750 some four thousand—mostly very small—commercial breweries had sprung up in Bavaria, all making excellent, mostly lager, beer. Every little village and hamlet had its own brewery, usually protected by local monopoly ordinances and supplying its tiny patch of the universe with brew. In some areas in Bavaria, the prohibition against drinking beer from another town remained in force until about two hundred years ago.

The political and economic victory of the bourgeoisie ultimately proved lasting, even in Bavaria. After the French Revolution (1789), rumblings of freedom were heard even in the most staunchly conservative and reactionary regions of Europe. In 1797, the French, imbued with democratic fervor, occupied the Rhineland, including Düsseldorf and Cologne. By 1806, Napoleon Bonaparte ruled most of Europe. In that year, the German Emperor, Francis II, who was also the king of Austria, resigned, and the Holy Roman Empire of the German Nation, which Otto I had founded in 962, was formally dissolved. According to Francis II, it was no longer worth governing.

The French Revolution:
Vive la Bière Libre

In an effort to maintain social control of the conquered Rhineland, the newly instated governor and brother-in-law to Napoleon, Joaquim Murat, forbade all trade and professional associations. This was the end of the brewers' guilds in Düsseldorf, Cologne, and most anywhere else in Germany.

Even in Bavaria, in the year 1800 local beer sale monopolies were abolished and every subject was allowed to drink whichever beer he wanted, even if it

Mug shot!

was from the next town instead of the local brewery. After 1805, country breweries were allowed to brew as much beer as their city competitors, and all breweries could own and operate brewpubs.

After the defeat of Napoleon at Waterloo (1815) and the peace treaty hammered out during the Vienna Congress that same year, the Rhineland became a province of Prussia. The Prussian rulers confirmed the abolition of the guilds, arguing that their rules of admission had been too restrictive. Henceforth, there was to be *Gewerbefreiheit,* the freedom of every Prussian subject to choose his own profession or trade unhampered by the closed-shop restrictions of the guilds. In the early nineteenth century protectionism in the beer business slowly fell by the wayside and competition became the rule. Brewing in most parts of Germany had become unshackled from its traditional limitations—except taxes, of course—and had been tossed into the treacherous waters of the open market. In Munich, for instance, in 1790 there were sixty breweries supplying the city's forty thousand inhabitants. By 1819 there were only thirty-five left, and by 1865 no more than fifteen. The marketplace eliminated inefficient enterprises, but those that survived the shakeout became bigger.

Brewing Turns Science

Freed from the constraints of religious dogma and feudal backwardness, critical free thought and scientific inquiry also took off. The changes in the intellectual world had started in the seventeenth century, after the Thirty Years' War, and had a profound impact on beer and brewing.

Since Sumerian and Egyptian times, beer had been made by spontaneous, uncontrolled fermentation. The ancients dropped a loaf of half-baked bread into a jar filled with water. They waited a few days, then took a straw and imbibed.

The monks, nuns, vassals, housewives, and craftsmen of the Middle Ages refined the techniques but still had no clue as to which processes they actually set in motion. The result of their efforts was, more often than not, an ale, rarely a lager, but the outcome was always chancy. Only with the rise of commercial freedom, intellectual enlightenment, and science and technology could beer making reach new heights. It was not until the nineteenth century that beer began to taste reliably and universally good.

To reach the level of proficiency of a modern brewer, someone had to figure out what actually happened in the fermenter. Brewers needed to see, to understand, and to control. That development took roughly from the start of the seventeenth to the end of the nineteenth centuries. It was driven by discovery and innovation, and within the span of a scant 250 years man moved from brewing by the seats of his pants to a scientific understanding and technological control of the processes required for beer quality and consistency.

From Putrefaction to Fermentation

Until the sixteenth century, government regulations like the *Reinheitsgebot* and the summer-brewing prohibition were the driving forces behind the changes in brewing practices, particularly in Bavaria. But even after 1516, when only barley, hops, and water were used, the result of the brewing process was still a matter of luck. Fermentation was commonly regarded as a mystical and spontaneous process, a form of putrefaction. The milky substance that settled out at the bottom of the fermenter or formed a flocculent layer at the top of the brew was not recognized for what it was (yeast). Instead, it was considered an impurity, a by-product of putrefaction that better be discarded. It was not known that this very "by-product" made alcoholic fermentation happen.

In practice, any number of airborne yeast strains, from lager yeasts *(Saccharomyces uvarum)* to ale yeasts *(Saccharomyces cerevisiae)* to wild yeasts, could be—and probably were—present in any given brew, and most likely all were infected with bacteria. Which yeast became dominant and defined the character of the beer depended largely on the ambient temperature. The warmer the cellar, the more likely that the beer would be an ale. Off-flavors in beer and a short shelf life were probably the rule rather than the exception, especially for beers brewed during the hot summer months. A theoretical understanding of the metabolism of yeast, of the differences between warm and cold fermenting yeasts—and of the differences between the beers they produce—had to wait until the late nineteenth century.

It was the German physician and chemist Andreas Libau, also known as Libavius (circa 1560–1616), who was the first to point out that fermentation and putrefaction were different processes. He knew about carbon dioxide (CO_2) and was the first to describe a method of distilling alcohol. It is doubtful that any brewer of Libavius's time read his heavy tome *Alchymia* (published in Latin in 1606), which was the first systematic textbook of chemistry, but later scientists did. Libavius laid the conceptual foundation for all subsequent discoveries about the true nature of fermentation.

I Can See Clearly Now

The Thirty Years' War had not only devastated central Europe physically, it also had brought most scientific work to a halt. Progress started to pick up only toward the eighteenth century, when the Age of Reason ushered in a new wave of intellectual, political, social, and economic change and propelled the Western world toward democracy, industrialization, and a secular lifestyle.

Although Antonie van Leeuwenhoek (1632–1723) appears to have had no interest in brewing, he was, without realizing it, the catalyst for the research that would ultimately solve the mystery of fermentation. Van Leeuwenhoek was a draper turned natural scientist and microscope maker. As a draper's apprentice in Amsterdam in 1648, young Antonie often had to check the quality of cloth under a lens. This helped spark his interest in optics. By 1871 he had constructed his first microscope. He assembled at least 242 of them in his lifetime, some with a magnification of as great as 270 times.

We know that Zacharias Janssen, a Dutch spectacle maker, had theorized about magnification before van Leeuwenhoek and had made a primitive model of the microscope around 1590 (as had Galileo in 1610), but van Leeuwenhoek's was the first truly usable device. In 1674 it helped him to see yeast cells, bacteria, and other protozoans (single-celled animals) as well as red blood cells for the very first time in history. He also described the reproduction of micro-organisms and thus refuted the theory of spontaneous generation, which to that time had furnished the accepted explanation for the cause of fermentation and putrefaction.

Finally, there was the yeast!

Controlling Time and Temperature

Have you ever thought what brewing would be like without a thermometer or even a clock? The invention of the first mechanical clock is credited to a learned monk, Gerbert, who later became Pope Sylvester II. His contraption dates from around 996, but mechanical clocks did not come into wider use until the late Middle Ages. Imagine controlling the mashing time or the boil in the brew kettle by keeping a watchful eye on an hourglass or maybe a sundial. Great variation in extract efficiency and beer quality must have been the order of the day when time was more a matter of guesswork than measurement.

The thermometer was not invented until a mere 250 years ago. The first usable thermometers were developed by a German named Daniel Gabriel Fahrenheit in 1714, by a Frenchman named René-Antoine Ferchault de Réaumur in 1731, and by a Swede named Anders Celsius in 1742. This new little gadget finally allowed brewers to control mash temperatures without having to mix fixed volumes of grain and water at either well temperature or at a boil.

Ethanol and CO_2

The French chemist Antoine-Laurent Lavoisier (1743–1794) made the next giant leap forward in fermentation knowledge. In 1789 he discovered that CO_2 and ethanol (a form of alcohol) are the products of alcoholic fermentation. He also explained the role of oxygen in the respiration of both plants and animals and thus contributed to our understanding of the carbon cycle that turns the barley on the stalk into the brew in our glass.

Lavoisier and the Perpetual Carbon Cycle

The French chemist Antoine-Laurent Lavoisier (1743–1794) supplied many of the building blocks of modern brewing science, but he himself was perhaps less interested in brewing beer than he was in studying the wonders of oxygen.

He was the first to discover that fire and combustion (the principle that makes our car engines run) are oxidation processes in which carbon and oxygen are combined to form carbon dioxide (CO_2). He also discovered that plant respiration is the opposite of oxidation. The plant reverses the process and separates carbon from oxygen. It keeps carbon particles for its own growth and releases oxygen into the air, where it becomes available for renewed oxidation.

For beer lovers, plant respiration is an important subject, because it is the first step in the conversion cycle that in the end yields up the refreshing glass of beer that our passion is all about.

The pigment, chlorophyll, in the leaves of green plants, including barley, is necessary in order for the plant to combine energy from the sun, CO_2 from the air, and water from the environment to form carbohydrates. For this purpose, plants use mostly the red and blue-violet portions of the visible spectrum of sunlight.

Green plants absorb CO_2 through stomates (pores in the skin of their leaves). They combine the carbon with water they get through their roots from the soil. The resulting carbohydrates occur primarily in the form of a type of sugar called glucose ($C_6H_{12}O_6$), as well as other sugars and starches. For easier storage, green plants convert some of the glucose to starch. This is the process brewers seek to reverse by activating sugar-converting *(diastatic)* enzymes during malting and mashing.

All green plants release oxygen during respiration, oxygen that animals need to breathe. The respiration process generally follows the chemical formula:

$$6CO_2 + 6H_2O = C_6H_{12}O_6 \text{ (glucose)} + 6O_2.$$

Carbohydrates serve as the building blocks for the plant's cells and tissues. Green plants develop special enzymes that convert some of these carbohydrates into such secondary products as fats and oils.

The carbon captured from the air by the green leaves can get passed along from one eater to the next, thus serving as the foundation of sometimes lengthy food chains. Depending on whether the carbohydrates stored in barley traveled through a cow or a yeast cell, they would wind up on your dinner table either as a steak or a glass of beer.

Plant respiration also generates certain by-products such as amino acids and organic acids. In addition, plants can synthesize proteins from nitrogen and other trace elements in the soil.

In brewing, we break down the direct and indirect products of respiration into nutrients suitable to be metabolized by the yeast during fermentation. The final products of this passage of carbon from the air through the barley, the mash, the kettle, and the yeast are carbon dioxide, alcohol, and residual sugars, the compounds that give beer effervescence, stability, and body.

Any excess CO_2 released into the atmosphere during fermentation may find its way back to a field of barley swaying in the breeze. There it may be trapped one fine sunny day by stomates—only to start the cycle all over again.

New Kiln—Clean Grain

After 1818 the taste of beer improved greatly as indirect hot-air kilning of malted grain gradually replaced the traditional direct-smoke kilning. Instead of sending hot, dirty smoke over the moist bed of malted grain, in an indirect system, the fuel heated a stream of clean air that was blown through the grain. Thus the grain no longer picked up smoky residues from coal or wood, flavors that used to be passed on to the beer. The new kilns also allowed for more precise temperature control of the drying grain and thus gave the brewer for the first time dependable pale malt as well as malt with predictable mashing qualities.

Who Done It? The Sugar Fungus!

By the beginning of the nineteenth century brewers knew that fermentation had nothing to do with rot, that yeast played an important role in brewing, and—thanks to Lavoisier—that fermentation produced alcohol and CO_2. Now it was time for someone to put it all together and explain the mechanisms at work in detail. Along came the German physiologist and histologist Theodor Schwann (1810–1882). Schwann discovered that the cell is the building block of all plant and animal tissue. He was also the first to recognize, in 1837, that the yeast cell, which was first seen by van Leeuwen-hoek under his microscope, is a living organism. Noting that the little critter had a sweet tooth, he called it "sugar fungus," hence the Latin name *Saccharomyces*. Schwann also discovered that the munching of sugars by *Saccharomyces,* which we call fermentation, occurs only when there is no air, namely, that fermentation is an anaerobic process.

Wort—How Sweet It Is

In 1843, only one year after the first Pilsner Urquell was brewed, the Bohemian chemist Carl Joseph Napoleon Balling invented the hydrometer. His gravity spindle measured the amount of dissolved substances in the wort—mostly sugars, but also proteins, minerals, vitamins, and aromatics— and thus allowed for the quantitative determination of extract strength and of the progress of fermentation (which brewers call *attenuation*).

Brewing science was finally getting somewhere! The milky by-product of medieval putrefaction had by now become firmly established as a living single-celled creature that converts sugars into alcohol and carbon dioxide and thus turns the brewer's wort into beer. Brewers could control the color of the grain that they fed the yeast, they could measure the yeast's temperature while it was at work in order to predict if they were producing a lager or an ale, and they could check the progress of the yeast's labors with a hydrometer. But if they wanted to tame the yeast, they had to find out what made it tick. The French chemist Louis Pasteur was the one to furnish that answer.

Aerobic and Anaerobic—The Double Life of Yeast

Louis Pasteur (1822–1895) became interested in the fermentation of wine, vinegar, and beer while he was a professor at universities in Dijon, Strasbourg, and Lille. By 1862 we find him at the *École normale* in Paris, where he is poised to finished off the myth of spontaneous fermentation for good. He discovered that heating liquid to about 145 °F (63 °C) for thirty minutes kills any bacteria or other organisms that it may contain (pasteurization), and that if the liquid is left hermetically sealed, no microbial activity—  spontaneous or otherwise—recurs. Always eager to increase the shelf life of their beers, breweries were among the first food and beverage industries to pasteurize their products.

Because infectants cannot suddenly appear in a sterile environment but must be introduced from the outside, Pasteur also admonished brewers to examine yeast cells under the microscope before adding them to the beer (pitching) in order to determine whether the yeast was infected or healthy.

In 1868 Pasteur moved to the Sorbonne. Two years later he was commissioned by the French government to investigate how French brewers could make a beer that could compete effectively against the rising flood of imports from Germany. Eight years later he spelled out his findings in his study *Études sur la bière,* which did not rescue the French beer market from domination by the neighboring Teutonic brew but did provide the most comprehensive explanation yet of the fermentation processes and the products that result from the yeast's metabolism.

He discovered that yeast metabolizes glucose (a type of sugar) under the presence of oxygen and that it uses energy gained from the sugar to grow and reproduce furiously. Under anaerobic conditions yeast does not grow much but, as Schwann had already observed, commences vigorous fermentation. This rule is now known as the Pasteur Effect: Oxygen suppresses fermentation; its absence stimulates it.

Since Pasteur we can manage the metabolic life of yeast through wort aeration after pitching and through subsequent oxygen starvation. We also know that if we start out with sterile wort and control the microbes we pitch into the brew, we can control the result and make good beer. Thanks to Pasteur, hygiene has become one of the most important tools in the brewer's repertoire.

Pure Beer from Pure Yeast

What was still needed was a practical way to segregate the different yeast strains and breed them pure. This problem was solved by the Danish botanist Emil Christian Hansen (1842–1909), a recognized authority on fungi *(Myces).* From 1879, Hansen worked as head of the laboratory of the Carlsberg Brewing Company in Copenhagen. He was the first, in 1881, to classify brewer's yeast into cold, bottom-fermenting lager strains *(Saccharomyces uvarum)* and warm, top-fermenting ale strains *(Saccharomyces cerevisiae).* All other yeasts are called "wild" in beer making and produce nasty off-flavors. *Saccharomyces uvarum,* incidentally, is also known as *Saccharomyces carlsbergensis.* It is not difficult to figure out where that name comes from.

Hansen also noted that within the two broad classes of beer-friendly top- and bottom-fermenting yeasts there are many variations, each with its own properties that affect the ultimate taste of the beer it ferments. Already in 1882 he demanded that yeast not only be free from bacteria, as Pasteur had insisted, but also free from "wild" yeast, if we want to make good beer. By 1890 he had developed a practical technique for the cultivation of pure yeast strains from a single cell. Pitching was never to be the same again.

And Enzymes, Too!

The British chemist Cornelius O'Sullivan was the first to figure out how enzymes work. As biochemical catalysts, enzymes convert, under the influence of moisture and warmth, unfermentable starches into fermentable sugars. O'Sullivan published his findings in 1890 and thus demystified the riddle of the mash. He supplied us with the last missing link in our understanding of the carbon chain's complex process by which the carbon dioxide in the air becomes the starch in the grain, the sugar in the wort, and finally the alcohol in the fermented beer.

There Is a Chill in the Wort

At this point, the biochemistry of both lager and ale fermentation was under control. But its practical application year-round still required a better way of controlling fermentation temperatures. By the middle of the nineteenth century it was clearly understood that yeast works best in a very narrow temperature range. Only then does it make beer with a good flavor. It was the invention of a German engineer, Carl von Linde, that finally allowed brewers to replace the traditional icehouses with mechanical refrigeration. The breakthrough came in 1873, when Linde, with the financial backing of Gabriel Sedlmayr, brewmaster at the Munich Spaten Brewery, completed his first working model of what was then called an "ammonia cold machine."

Linde recognized that when a compressed gas is permitted to expand or a solid is liquefied, heat is absorbed from the surroundings.

Ammonia, CO_2, freon, or several other volatile chemicals can be used as refrigerants as long as they lend themselves to alternating condensation and evaporation in a closed system. Linde used an electric motor to compress gaseous ammonia into a liquid. He then released it into the coils of a refrigeration compartment. There the ammonia reverted to its gaseous form and in the process drew heat from its environment. The motor then repeated the cycle by converting the ammonia gas back into a liquid, and so on and so on. Compression is best done away from the refrigerated area, because compression gives off heat.

Different people, including Linde, have been credited with the invention of refrigeration, but it was Linde's work with the new technology and the enthusiastic support of brewmaster Sedlmayr that led to the universal embrace of refrigeration by the brewing industry. To this day the compressors and evaporators in a modern brewery still work according to the same principles that Linde used in his first cold machine.

Filtration and Air-Free Draft Beer

In 1878 Lorenz Enzinger, a Bavarian living in Worms on the banks of the Rhine River, put a filtration device on the market that took yeast and other suspended solids out of beer before it was packaged. This gave beer clarity and a longer shelf life. Two years later the first patented machine for dispensing beer with CO_2 instead of air appeared. Then even draft beer stayed fresh to the last drop.

Brewery Suppliers Follow Suit

Advances in such areas as water chemistry, grain and hops botany, metallurgy, thermodynamics, and packaging technology all contributed to enhancements in the quality of beer. Grain botany gave us laboratory-bred barley of high enzymatic power, low levels of protein, and a minimum of resinous and phenolic off-flavors. Hop breeders developed varieties with specific bittering (alpha acid) ranges and aroma oils. Improved malting techniques gave us better control over beer color and flavor and the enzymatic properties of brewing grains. New mash tun, brew kettle, and fermenter designs allowed for perfect temperature control, high extract efficiency, and wort sterility.

The first freight ever transported on a German railroad: two kegs of beer (what else), in 1836.

Finally: Modern Beer!

Although most of the developments described above improved the quality of both ales and lagers, it was Hansen's and Linde's pioneering work, which occurred only a little more than a hundred years ago, that made the modern lager revolution possible. As we have seen in previous chapters, brewers certainly had made lager beers before then. However, because fermentation was carried out by mixed yeast cultures and—without refrigeration—at relatively high temperatures, the "default" beer made by most of our forefathers was usually an ale. The best lagers were made mostly during the winter months and then only in cooler regions when and where nature was cooperative. Thanks to science and technology, by the end of the nineteenth century brewers were able to brew ales and lagers anywhere with predictable quality.

Within a scant two decades from von Linde's invention of refrigeration, the conversion of German breweries from top fermentation to bottom fermentation was complete—except in the Rhineland. But even there the commercial production of modern ales is plainly unthinkable without the use of pure, laboratory-managed, bacteria-free *Saccharomyces cerevisiae* or without rigid temperature control of the mash and the fermenting wort.

Advances in technology, especially of steam generation and refrigeration, also made brewing more capital-intensive, and many small breweries folded or were taken over in Germany (and in the rest of the world) as industrialization, with its large-scale factory breweries, arrived in the

Courtesy of Privatbrauerei Hoepfner, Karlsruhe, Germany.

Before the invention of refrigeration, breweries used blocks of ice to keep their fermentation cellars cool. This wintery picture from 1886/1887 shows the Hoepfner Brewery of Karlsruhe's 4,000-ton stock pile of ice. To keep the ice mountain from melting during the heat of summer, it was covered with peat moss.

nineteenth century. Breweries could expand their markets beyond the local horizon as the railway quickly replaced the horse-drawn dray for beer transport. In fact, the very first freight ever transported by a German railway was two casks of beer brewed by the Lederer Brewery of Nürnberg! The casks traveled to Fürth on July 11, 1836, on the first German rail link a mere seven months after it had been opened.

To be sure, there are even today small local breweries owned by nobles, convents, monasteries, or private individuals, but these do not account for a large share of the output of the German beer industry. Munich, for instance, boasted some sixty-seven breweries in 1750. Within a century and a half this number shrank to just a few large ones, such as Augustiner, Hacker-Pschorr, Löwenbräu, Paulaner-Salvator-Thomasbräu, Spaten-Franziskanerbräu, and Staatliches Hofbräuhaus. More than half the beer brewed in Bavaria now comes from a handful of these large corporations.

In Cologne there were still about 120, mostly small, ale breweries in 1860. There were about one hundred in Düsseldorf. By the end of the First World War, however, only about half remained in the two cities, and of those, fewer than half were small craft brewpubs. By the end of the Second World War, only twenty-one breweries survived in Cologne, incidentally the same number that started Cologne's Fraternity of Brewers in 1438. Today the number of kölsch breweries has rebounded slightly to twenty-four. In Düsseldorf, eighteen breweries survived the destruction of the Second World War. Of those, only two large ones and four brewpubs have weathered the mergers of the last few decades.

According to a *Boston Globe* report of October 1996, there are about twelve hundred breweries left in Germany, but their numbers are declining. More than 130 closed between 1990 and 1995 alone.

However, the Germans' love affair with beer is far from over. German breweries still produce a staggering 115 million hectoliters (almost 100 million barrels) a year, and each German still drinks about 140 liters (about 37 gallons) of the stuff each year (statistical average for 1995). By comparison, Americans manage to down about 85 liters (22 gallons) a year.

Beer is still the anchor of popular culture in Germany. There is hardly a country in the world with so many drinking songs. And they are still being sung! Just visit a German pub during Mardi Gras, which is called *Fasching* in the south, *Fassenacht* in Hesse, and *Karneval* in the north, and you can watch the otherwise serious and reserved Germans loosen up over a mug of suds. In the beer halls of the land it is quite customary for strangers to share long tables, to join arms, and to sway together from side to side in a jovial sing-along.

When entering a German pub or restaurant you do not wait to be seated, as you would in North America. Germans are—perhaps surprisingly—social eaters and drinkers. Whereas in North America, restaurant patrons expect to be seated separately, and every party of one or party of two has a table that might actually seat four, Germans pick their own seating in restaurants, often preferring vacant seats at an already occupied table to the solitude of single dining.

Among the younger crowd you may still encounter the custom of *Stiefeltrinken* ("boot drinking"). A glass boot, containing one or two liters of beer, makes the rounds at a large table nonstop from one occupant to another. Each drinker takes turns placing the tip of the boot in the air and taking a careful sip. As the beer level gets closer and closer to the boot's ankle, air is sucked into the tip, displacing the beer that is there and splattering the drinker's face. The object of the game is to avoid getting splashed by quickly twisting the tip of the boot downward as soon as the air begins to rush in—without taking one's mouth off the rim of the boot. Anybody who misses the moment and does get splashed has to order (and pay for) the next boot. Obviously, those who are clever at this game can imbibe with their friends all night without spending a penny. Indeed,

if you watch carefully you can still detect in modern Germans assembled in a pub or beer hall a bit of the tribal frolicker that the Roman historian Tacitus described so well some two thousand years ago.

These boots are made for drinking . . .

Brewer: An Honest Profession for a King

America has George Washington and Samuel Adams, two great ale-brewing leaders. Germany has Frederick II (1712–1786), known to history as the Great, ruler of Prussia, flutist, composer—and apprenticed ale brewer.

As a young lad Frederick liked to withdraw to his study and indulge in his passion for poetry and philosophy, quite to the disgust of his coarse and tyrannical father, Frederick Wilhelm I, known to all as the "soldier-king." The dislike between the two men was mutual, but Daddy had the power to impose his will.

To prepare his son for the crass world of politics and statesmanship, he decreed that the crown prince had better learn a real profession. He sent the future sovereign off to Küstrin, a small town at the confluence of the Warthe and Oder Rivers on the Polish side of the present-day border between Germany and Poland. There the king apprenticed his son to a brewer.

Frederick Wilhelm I was a consummate admirer of the brew and was eager to pass his passion on to the delicate young lad. "I order," wrote the king to the Küstrin brewmaster, "to give him all the necessary instruction in the brewing enterprise and to show him how to handle the brew, treat the mash, place the brew in the vats, put it in casks, and all the other things that need to be done, including how malt is prepared and how one can tell if it is good" (Hellex 1981).

For once, a father's pedagogical strategy bore fruit. Young Frederick never forgot the experience and remained an ardent protector of the brewing industry throughout his reign. On one occasion he decided that the Prussians were consuming too much coffee, the importation of which was draining the kingdom's scarce monetary reserves. He simply forbade the importation of the bitter bean. His justification: "Every farmer and common man is now getting used to coffee. This has to be restricted so that the people become used to beer again, for this is in the best interest of our own breweries. It is my intention that not so much money leaves the country in exchange for coffee. By the way, your royal majesty himself has been raised on beer soup, which is much healthier than coffee. His fathers have known only beer, and this is a beverage that suits our climate" (Hellex 1981).

Frederick II ("The Great") of Prussia enjoyed the finer things of life: flute playing, composing, philosophizing—and brewing. Here he is the soloist in a flute concert in his salon in Berlin.

chapter 10

Beer Making
for the Uninitiated

■ ■ ■ ■ ■ ■ ■ ■ ■ ■ ■ ■ ■ ■ ■ ■ ■ ■ ■

𝔍f you are one of those people who can already talk with great felicity about such subjects as proteolytic conversion or isomerization of alpha acids, feel free to skip the next few pages. We'll meet you again in the next chapter.

For the rest, who may not have a clue what these five-dollar words mean, no need to worry. It's the end product of the brewing process—the beer—that delights the soul. Leave it to the brewer to know the chemical and microbiological details. However, if you are curious about what goes on in a brew house, here is a brief, no-nonsense summary in plain English.

Filter Coffee, Soup, and Leavening

If you know how to brew filter coffee, boil soup, and let bread dough rise, you have a basic understanding of the beer-making process.

The first step in beer making is called *mashing*. This involves the steeping of milled grain in hot water to activate enzymes. These convert the grain's large proteins into smaller ones and the grain's unfermentable starches into fermentable sugars.

After mashing, the brewer tries to separate the sugars he has created from the solid grain. As with a coffee filter, the brewer sprinkles *(sparges)* hot water over the grain bed to leach out *(lauter,* from the German word *läutern,* "to purify") a malty-sweet extract into the brew kettle. The initial running of the extract is very rich, but as the brewer continues to sparge, the extract becomes thinner and thinner. The brewer stops the sparge when the sugar content of the blended extract (called *wort)* in the kettle is just right. The spent grain, like spent coffee grounds, is then discarded. It often becomes a nutritious feed for cattle.

The brewer then boils the wort in the kettle. This process is more like making a pot of soup. At the beginning of the boil the brewer adds hops. Like the goodness in a soup bone, the bittering compounds of the hops (called alpha acids) must be leached out and changed by the boiling liquid. This process is called *isomerization*. At the end of the boil the brewer adds another charge of hops, this time for flavor and aroma. Although the bittering substances have to be extracted from the hops by a vigorous boil, the flavor and aroma compounds in hops are volatile and remain in the brew only if they are added late enough so that they do not have a chance to escape into the air.

Other important processes occur during the boil. Undesirable coagulants such as vegetable gums and large-molecule proteins that are leached out of the grain in the mash tun flocculate in the hot wort. What happens in the kettle is similar to the cooking of an egg dropped into boiling soup. These coagulants, as well as nonsoluble plant matter from the hops, finally settle to the bottom of the kettle, where they form a layer of *trub* (from the German word *trübe,* "murky"). The clear wort can then be siphoned off above the trub. The wort is then force-cooled through a heat exchanger or, rarely nowadays, allowed to cool in flat vats, before it is pumped into the fermenter.

The fermenter usually contains the yeast. It was put there *(pitched)* by the brewer before the transfer of the cold wort. Yeasts are single-celled organisms that absorb sugars for energy and release alcohol, carbon dioxide gas, and several trace elements as by-products of their metabolism. In bread dough yeast does the same job, but the carbon dioxide gas is trapped and causes the dough to rise. In beer, the brewer initially allows the carbon dioxide to escape, but near the end of the fermentation period, when the beer is almost completely *attenuated* (when most sugars have been converted to alcohol and carbon dioxide), the brewer can close the fermenter and chill the brew. The yeast continues to produce carbon dioxide, but the gas has no place to go and remains in suspension in the beer—to be released only when we pour the beer into a glass.

From a brewer's perspective, there are wild yeasts, which spoil beer, and there are brewer's yeasts, which do a delicious job. Today, there are hundreds of pure strains of brewer's yeast available, each with

its special flavor characteristics. As we have seen, all brewer's yeasts fall into two basic categories, *Saccharomyces cerevisiae,* which makes ales, and *Saccharomyces uvarum,* which makes lagers. It is the yeast, and nothing but the yeast, that determines if a beer is an ale or a lager. That's it.

When you walk into a brewery's fermentation area you can tell immediately which beer is being made there. Ale yeast makes the best-tasting beers when it is allowed to ferment the wort at room temperature, whereas lager yeast works best at a cool cellar temperature. Therefore, if you feel comfortable, the brewery makes ales; if there is a chill in the air that makes you hanker for a sweater, it makes lagers.

After fermentation, the beer is usually filtered to remove any remaining suspended particulates, including yeast cells. The clear finished beer is then ready to be packaged into bottles and kegs.

The Ways of the English, the Ways of the Germans

English and German brewers use essentially the same steps to make their brews. But why are the results so different? Here are some of the reasons.

Hops

The Latin taxonomic name for hops, *Humulus lupulus,* means wolf plant. It is a vine that is related to the nettle and to cannabis (hemp), the source of marijuana. Hops contain bittering substances, called alpha acids or *humulones,* and flavor substances, called beta acids or *lupulones.* In addition, they contain volatile aroma oils. Like grapes, hops are rich in tannins. The acids and tannins also preserve the beer and increase its keeping qualities on the shelf.

English beers are usually made with hop varieties that are high in alpha acids. These are generally more astringent than the continental European varieties and contribute a fruity to floral, even to peppery, flavor to the brew. Famous English ale hops are Kent Golding and Fuggles.

German beers, on the other hand, are generally made with so-called noble hop varieties. Their bitterness tends to be more gentle but nonetheless spicy, even pungent, and their flavor and aroma are mellow and lingering. The most common hop varieties that are generally considered "noble" are Hallertau, Tettnang, and Spalt from Germany, and Saaz from the Czech Republic.

Mashing English-Style

In the mash tun, English wort is generally extracted from what is called a single-step infusion mash. Hot water is infused into the grain to bring the mix of water and milled grain (the mash) to a temperature of about 150–154 °F (66–68 °C). At this temperature, special enzymes (called *diastatic enzymes)* that are naturally in the grain become active and convert grain starches into simple sugars such as glucose, maltose, and fructose. This is called the *sugar rest.* Simple sugars are fully fermentable by all yeast strains. The enzymes also produce *melibiose,* a sugar that can be fermented by most lager yeasts but never by ale yeasts, so it therefore stays in the beer. This fact contributes to the different tastes of ales and lagers. Enzymes work similarly to the catalytic converter in your car. They cause chemical changes to happen but are not part of the new compounds that are formed. Enzymes are nature's organic catalysts.

After the sugar rest, the English brewer brings his mash quickly to the "mash-out" temperature of about 170 °F (77 °C), which is high enough to dissolve sugars easily in the runoff but low enough not to leach unconverted starches or off-flavor substances such as phenols out of the grain bed. Grains grown in the maritime climate of the British Isles tend to be low in proteins. The proteins that do get dragged into the wort during sparging tend to coagulate out during the boil in the brew kettle. If they didn't, they could cause a haze in the finished beer, especially if the beer is stored cold. Unconverted starches, too, can turn cold beer murky. Cloudiness in cold beer is called a *chill haze.*

Mashing German-Style

German beers generally undergo a more complicated mash tun regimen than do English beers. Grains grown in the continental climate of central Europe tend to be richer in proteins than British grains. This may

be great for making a nutritious bread, but it creates a problem for the brewer who tries to make a crisp, haze-free lager.

Fortunately, nature has provided the brewer with a special set of enzymes, called *proteolytic enzymes,* that reside in the kernel of the grain and are active at temperatures between approximately 113 and 131 °F (45 and 55 °C). These enzymes break down large-chain high-molecular-weight proteins that tend to form chill hazes into smaller-chain proteins that don't. These converted proteins have such fancy names as albumins, peptides, and polypeptides.

To accomplish this proteolytic conversion, the German brewer must mash in at a much lower temperature than the English brewer would in order to give the special proteolytic enzymes a chance to do their job. The time of their labor is called the *protein rest*. The brewer achieves this by initially infusing the grain with very little hot water *(doughing-in)* to create a thick mash for the protein rest and by then infusing the mash a second time with hot water to bring the grain bed to the next temperature step for the sugar rest. The entire process is called *step mashing*.

Traditional breweries also use a so-called *decoction method* for step mashing. After the protein rest, a certain portion of the mash, usually about one-third, is drawn off, boiled in a separate kettle, and then reintroduced to the main mash. The result is an increase in temperature of the entire mash to the next level. In addition to raising the temperature, decoction also duplicates some of the work of the proteolytic and diastatic enzymes. It breaks down proteins and converts starches to sugars. For grain varieties with few enzymes, therefore, decoction—rather than infusion—is a must if the brewer wants to achieve authentic German beer.

Modern plant breeding, however, has created special strains of low-protein brewing grains, and technological improvements in malt kilning has resulted in highly modified grains, that is, grains of exceptional enzymatic strength. Many continental breweries, therefore, have abandoned traditional decoction mashing in favor of step-infusion mashing.

The sugar rest, too, is often more complicated in a German as compared to an English beer. Some of the diastatic enzymes in the grain become active at a temperature of roughly 158–167 °F (70–75 °C). These enzymes produce complex sugars, such as dextrins, that generally cannot be metabolized by the yeast and thus stay in the finished beer. German brewers often have a separate infusion or decoction cycle to stimulate the production of these complex sugars.

Proteins and Dextrins, the Invisible Web

To humans, the converted proteins and complex sugars in beer are completely tasteless. Texture, not flavor, is their most important function in beer. They add body and mouthfeel to brews that might otherwise be perceived as too thin and weak, or, to use the technical term, "dry," which means beer without residual sugars.

Proteins and dextrins also form an invisible web in the beer through which carbon dioxide bubbles must work their way slowly to the surface. As a result, beer with lots of body remains effervescent longer and its bubbles remain smaller, as happens in Champagne. The carbon dioxide bubbles do not combine into large pockets of burpy gas, as happens in carbonated mineral water, a drink with no body whatsoever.

Once carbon dioxide bubbles reach the surface of a beer with body, they drag part of the invisible web out of the brew. Exposed to air, the proteins and dextrins form the rich, creamy, long-lasting head for which German beers are so famous.

The Miracle of Lagering

German beers stay in the fermenter at least twice as long as do English beers, and invariably at lower temperatures, provided, of course, that the yeast strain is comfortable at the selected temperature range. In general, the lower the fermentation temperature, the slower the fermentation and the smaller the amount of off-flavors released by the yeast. These off-flavors come mostly from sulfuric and buttery-tasting fermentation by-products.

Prolonged lagering (cold-storing, from the German word *lagern,* "to store") of the fermented beer has the added effect of allowing the yeast to reabsorb through its cell membrane many of the unpleasant-tasting by-products of its own metabolism. In a sense, the yeast "scrubs" the beer clean, which is the true miracle of beer maturation through lagering. Note that in Germany, *both* ales and lagers are "lagered." A German beer that has been lagered for about four to six weeks—that is, aged on the yeast near the freezing point—will taste very clean, soft, and mellow indeed.

The guiding principle for making quality German beer authentically is "easy does it." This involves processes that are comparatively more labor-intensive and capital-intensive than those employed by most breweries making English ales. These processes also differ from the techniques used to brew the mass-produced factory imitations of German-style or Bohemian-style lagers that are Pilseners or premium lagers in name only. In an age where economics dictate ever-faster production cycles and where the pressure for maximum profit governs what we make industrially, it is refreshing to know that the traditional breweries of the Old World as well as the microbreweries of the New World can still make both quality beers and a profit.

Those readers who wish to delve into the more technical aspects of brewing are encouraged to consult *Principles of Brewing Science,* by George Fix, and *New Brewing Lager Beer,* by Gregory Noonan. Both books are published by Brewers Publications in Boulder, Colorado (see References and Further Reading).

chapter 11

Brewing in Style

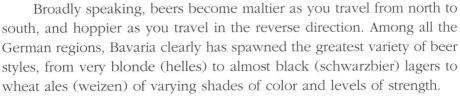

ermans are very conscious of distinct beer styles. When they order a beer, they rarely ask for it by its brand name. Rather, they order beer by its style designation, asking for a Pils, alt, kölsch, weizen, helles, or dunkel.

German beer making has taken different paths in different parts of the country. Thus, Germans associate different beer styles with different regions, though virtually all beer styles are now available anywhere in modern Germany.

Broadly speaking, beers become maltier as you travel from north to south, and hoppier as you travel in the reverse direction. Among all the German regions, Bavaria clearly has spawned the greatest variety of beer styles, from very blonde (helles) to almost black (schwarzbier) lagers to wheat ales (weizen) of varying shades of color and levels of strength.

Neighboring Bohemia (now part of the Czech Republic) has produced, under Bavarian influence, the world's most popular style, the Pilsner, which is the mother of all modern lagers.

The Rhineland and Westphalia, which together now form the state of North Rhine–Westphalia, probably rank second in contributions to the

German beer landscape. The Rhineland, with its alt and kölsch ales, has become the custodian of the ancient German ale tradition, whereas Westphalia has enriched the world with its peculiar interpretation of the blonde lager, the Dortmunder export.

The northern regions, until the late Middle Ages hotbeds of ale brewing, have given us the dry, assertively hoppy Pils, the original bock from Einbeck, and a light, acidic wheat beer called Berliner weisse.

"When I grow up, I want to be a stein just like you."

A Myriad of Brands

Within these broad guidelines, German breweries produce an endless array of both lagers and ales. This book seeks to explore the origin and variety of German beer styles, not the staggering variety of beer brands. If you are interested in a consumer's guide with brand-by-brand analyses of beers, there are several great reference works available that cover beers from all around the world, including Germany. Particularly noteworthy are Michael Jackson's *The New World Guide to Beer, The Simon and Schuster Pocket Guide to Beer, Michael Jackson's Beer Companion,* and Roger Protz's *The Ultimate Encyclopedia of Beer.* These books contain a wealth of insights that their itinerant authors have amassed over decades of informed sampling. You can obtain these books in most homebrew supply stores and better bookstores. The Jackson books are available directly from the Association of Brewers: P.O. Box 1679, Boulder, Colorado 80306-1679. An excellent technical book on brewing different beer styles is *Designing Great Beers,* by Ray Daniels. It is published by Brewers Publications, a division of the Association of Brewers, in Boulder.

The German Tax Collector's Classification of Beers

Though there are a dozen or so major beer styles in Germany, the official beer classification by the German tax collector lists only four types, none of which has anything to do with flavor.

German breweries pay tax depending on the extract strength of their wort. "Extract" refers to the nonwater compounds that are in solution in the wort. These are malt sugars, proteins, minerals, vitamins, acids, tannins, aromatic oils, and other trace elements leached out of the grain and the hops during the mash and the boil. It is measured as a percentage of 1,000 grams (about 1 liter) of wort. For instance, if 120 of 1,000 grams of unfermented wort are made up of substances other than water, the taxman considers this a 12% extract beer. The government allows for these four categories of extract:

Revenue Category	Extract Strength	Market Share
Einfachbier (simple beer)	2–5.5%	0.1%
Schankbier (draft beer)	7–8%	0.2%
Vollbier (whole beer)	11–14%	99%
Starkbier (strong beer)	16–28%	0.7%

Note how the scale is not continuous. The German tax authorities, for some unintelligible reason, do not recognize the existence of beers with, for instance, 15% extract. Hey, just because something is official does not mean it has to make sense!

German brewers have made their peace with this classification. They had to, else they could not have stayed in business. Ninety-nine percent of all beer made in Germany is *Vollbier* with an extract value of 11–14%.

From a historical perspective, beers outside these government ranges would be no less authentic, provided they were made true to style. German-style beers made by microbreweries in North America are, of course, not shackled by these bureaucratic irrelevancies and can be perfectly valid examples of the glory of German brews, even if they do not meet the exact extract criteria of the modern German tax collector.

It is a common mistake to think that there is a direct connection between the extract strength of wort and the alcoholic strength of the beer made from it. Not so, because several of the substances in solution in the wort are unfermentable, that is, they cannot be converted by the yeast into alcohol but contribute to the beer's body. Also, some of the carbon atoms in the malt sugars are lost as carbon dioxide gas during fermentation and thus do not add to the beer's alcoholic strength. As a practical rule of thumb, however, in most beers about one-third to one-fourth of the extract is converted by the yeast into alcohol. Thus, a 12% extract beer may yield about 3–4% alcohol by weight (abw), which translates into about 3.5–5% alcohol by volume (abv).

The "Real" Classification of Beer

Didn't Winston Churchill say that democracy is the most rotten form of government—except for all the others? The common person may not be perfect but on average probably has a better understanding of a subject than does an appointed government official, especially when it comes to enjoyment. Although the German government considers 99% of beers *Vollbier* and splits hairs by trying to fit the remaining 1% into three categories, the common imbiber has a much more meaningful handle on the classification of beers. His palate understands style. He has no trouble telling the difference between an alt, a weizen, and a Pils immediately, though they are all *Vollbier* to the bureaucrat. There are just different beers for different moods and different occasions. On a hot summer afternoon, for example, the lazy quaffer may crave a helles to keep his internal temperature in check, while on a wintry afternoon he may crave a tankard of nourishing doppelbock to warm his insides and help him forget the frosty punishment he endured earlier, while he was waiting for his commuter bus.

Many a German intuitively knows about the artistry of beer. He knows that when the brewer makes up his grain bill, selects his hops, and picks his yeast, what he creates is a *style*. Now let him create his variation on a theme by changing the ingredients and processes a little bit, though still adhering to some basic guidelines, and what we get is a brand in that particular style. In the following chapters we shall examine some of the German beer styles in greater detail.

Originally, beer coasters in Germany were plain round or square drip catchers made of felt. Once soiled, these mats could be washed and dried for reuse. A more upscale version of the beer coaster was made of white ceramic with a hollow in the center to keep the cool beer glass from resting in a puddle of condensate. By about 1880, pubs started to use round or square coasters made of cardboard. Breweries soon noticed the advertising potential of coasters and started to print their names and logos on them, first in one color and on one side only. Since the 1950s, breweries have been using beer coasters of all shapes and in all colors of the rainbow, with messages printed on both sides.

German Beer Styles at a Glance

The following is a brief summary of the major German beer styles, in alphabetical order and with their key characteristics. Please note that all extract and alcohol ranges are approximate and pay no heed to the German tax designations. Alcohol ranges are in alcohol by volume, not weight.

Alt

An ale. Extract 11-12%; alcohol 4-5%. Copper-colored, moderate to assertive hop bitterness, aromatic, full-bodied, cold-conditioned, malty finish.

Berliner Weisse

An ale. Extract 7–8%; alcohol about 3%. Pale wheat beer, very little hop bitterness, highly effervescent, fruity, tart, very sour, and therefore usually mixed (in the glass) with raspberry or woodruff-flavored syrup.

Bock

A lager. Extract 16–18%; alcohol 6–6.5%. Pale or dark, full-bodied, substantial mouthfeel, aromatic, mild hop bitterness, malty finish.

Doppelbock

A lager. Extract above 18%; alcohol 6.5–7.5%. Pale or dark, full-bodied, very substantial mouthfeel, little hop bitterness, pronounced malty finish.

Dortmunder

See export.

Dunkel

A lager. Extract 12–14%; alcohol 5–6%. The original Bavarian lager: dark brown, mild hop bitterness, full-bodied, very malty.

Eisbock

A lager. Extract up to 28%; alcohol 9–11%. Dark, very full-bodied, little hop bitterness, pronounced malty to sweet aromatic finish. Germany's strongest brew.

Export

A lager. Extract 12–14%; alcohol 4.5–5.5%. Pale, moderate hop bitterness, full-bodied, malt aroma. Local name for Dortmunder.

Hefeweizen

See Weizen/Weissbier.

Helles

A lager. Extract 11–12%; alcohol 4–5%. Pale golden, very mild hop bitterness, soft, full-bodied, malt aroma.

Kölsch

An ale. Extract 11–12%; alcohol 4–5%. Pale, moderate to assertive hop bitterness, full-bodied, cold-conditioned, crisp finish.

Kristallweizen

See Weizen/Weissbier.

Malzbier

An ale. Extract 12–14%; alcohol 1–2%. Dark, rich, malty, full-bodied, very sweet; enriched with caramelized, unfermentable sugar syrup. Often a kid's beer.

Märzen

A lager. Extract 12.4–14%; alcohol 4.5–5%. Amber to deep golden, mild hop bitterness, full-bodied, malt aroma, slightly sweet finish. Same as Oktoberfest.

Oktoberfest

See Märzen.

Pils/Pilsener

A lager. Extract 11–12%; alcohol 4–5%. Blonde, effervescent, assertively bitter upfront kick, dry and hoppy finish; some malty notes in southern German brews, exceptionally hoppy and spicy notes in the northern and eastern German brews. Germany's most popular beer style.

Pilsner

A lager. Extract 11–12%; alcohol 4–5.5%. The original modern lager from the Czech Republic. Deep blonde, fruitier than its German cousins, effervescent, lingering malty and aromatic finish.

Rauchbier

A lager. Extract 13–14%; alcohol about 5.5%. Dark, spicy, "bacony," moderate hop bitterness, full-bodied, malty, very smoky finish.

Schwarzbier

A lager. Extract 12–14%; alcohol 4.5%–5.5%. Dark, mild hop bitterness, full-bodied, malty but never toasty finish.

Vienna

See Wiener.

Weizen/Weissbier

An ale. Extract 11–14%; alcohol 4.5–5.5%. Pale (hell) or dark (dunkel), clear (kristallweizen) or yeast-turbid (hefeweizen), very effervescent, notes of spicy cloves, mild hop bitterness, malty or banana-fruity finish.

Weizenbock

An ale. Extract 16–17%; alcohol 6–7%. Pale, strong wheat beer, moderate hop bitterness, malt aroma.

Weizendoppelbock

An ale. Extract 18–19%; alcohol 6.5%–7.5%. Pale, strong wheat beer, moderate hop bitterness, pronounced malt aroma.

Wiener

A lager. Extract 12.4–14%; alcohol 4.5–5%. Amber to deep golden, mild hop bitterness, slightly sweet finish. Similar to Märzen, but usually less body and less malty.

chapter 12

German Ale Styles

■ ■ ■ ■ ■ ■ ■ ■ ■ ■ ■ ■ ■ ■ ■ ■ ■ ■ ■

In modern Düsseldorf it's still chic to imbibe an age-old brew, the alt, whose origins date to the beginning of civilization. *Alt* in German means old—an allusion to the old style of brewing, before lager.

It is somehow fitting that it should be Düsseldorf that has become the guardian of the old German ale tradition. After all, it was in the Neanderthal, a bare 10 miles east of the city where in 1858 the skeletal remains of the first known Neanderthal man were unearthed. He and his clan, all precursors of our present *Homo sapiens,* roamed the Rhineland some 50,000 to 100,000 years ago. A lot has happed in Düsseldorf since that time, but the city has somehow managed to integrate its heritage with its future.

Do not be surprised to find a dapper and suave young gentleman sitting on a stool in a ritzy bar on the *Königsallee* (king's alley), Düsseldorf's version of New York's Fifth Avenue or Paris's *Champs élysées,* sipping his alt from a straight-sided 0.2-liter glass as he tries to put the make on an equally well turned out young lady.

In the city's *Altstadt* (old town), known affectionately as the longest bar in the world because almost every building within a square mile contains a pub—there are about two hundred of them—you ask for a beer and what you get is an alt. If you want a Pils or a helles, you've got to ask for it specifically. Many of the buildings in the *Altstadt* date from the thirteenth to the seventeenth centuries. There you find three of the four alt beer meccas, the brewpubs that have defined the style for our age, *Uerige, Im Füchschen,* and *Zum Schlüssel.* The other mecca, *Schumacher,* is located on the Oststraße, about a mile to the east of the *Altstadt.* One old tavern, *Zum Schiffchen,* has been in business since 1628 and was Napoleon's watering hole when he stopped in the city in 1811 during his takeover of Europe.

However, the old-style beer has held its own not only in Düsseldorf: The folks in the shadow of that famous ancient cathedral 44 kilometers up the Rhine from Düsseldorf, who are rooted in the same brewing traditions, developed their own version of "old" beer. The people of Cologne, known equally for their pride in all things local and for their abhorrence of anything Düsseldorfian, could not name their "old" beer alt. That name had already been appropriated by those stuck-up Düsseldorfers downstream. So they simply named it kölsch, after their own town of Köln (Cologne in English). Today the name kölsch is legally protected similarly to an *appellation d'origine contrôllée* of a French wine, and it may be applied only to top-fermented beers brewed in the city limits of Cologne and by a few breweries on the immediate outskirts—twenty-four breweries in all. The brewers of Cologne (and the Berliner weisse brewers of Berlin, incidentally) enjoy what is probably the only beer appellation in the world. Among the more famous smaller breweries of Cologne are Früh, Sion, Päffgen, Töller, and Malzmühle. There are a few midsize breweries as well, but the five largest kölsch breweries nowadays produce almost two-thirds of all kölsch beer.

Cologne Burghers—Fierce Defenders of the Ale

In the Middle Ages Cologne had risen to become the proud center of the Rhineland. A Roman fort since 38 B.C., it was the residence of an archbishop with an impressive Gothic cathedral under construction. Cologne was a hub of commerce, with trading connections up and down the Rhine and even to London. What's more, unlike that of southern Germany, the local barley ale, flavored with hops or *gruit,* was good and profitable.

In 1438 the city's twenty-one breweries organized the Fraternity of Brewers to orchestrate collective action in defense of the local brew. At about this time there were threats on the horizon from imported

Keutebiers (wheat beers) from such well-known brew centers as Dortmund in Westphalia, and Hamburg at the North Sea.

Keutebiers started to undercut the preeminence of the local barley-based ale, and the Cologne city fathers, fearing for their revenues, forbade the importation of these beers, but to no avail. The populace continued to clamor for wheat beer and, as should be expected, smuggling flourished. Finally the city authorities caved in, and some Cologne brewers were allowed to make a beer similar to the import, but until 1471 these brewers were denied membership in the Fraternity. By 1500, however, the Fraternity relaxed its rules and the membership grew to eighty-nine breweries, all of which made both hopped barley-based ale and *Keutebier*. By that time, *gruit* beer, flavored with herbs and spices, had become outlawed in Cologne.

By 1555, the harmony between the breweries and the city authorities of Cologne was shattered—over the tax issue, of course. The city council announced that, henceforth, the brew privilege belonged exclusively to the authorities. From then on, burgher-brewers had to make their beer in a common city brew house under the supervision of two city-appointed brewmasters. Many brew burghers decided to close shop rather than submit to the caprice of the city officials, and the number of private breweries in Cologne declined quickly to about sixty-five.

The city council not only restricted who could brew but, again, what could be brewed. In 1603 they issued an important mandate: Only top-fermented beer, the forerunner of the modern kölsch ale, could be produced in Cologne. Some nine decades after the *Reinheitsgebot* had become the law in Bavaria and pushed that part of Germany firmly into the lager column, the authorities in Cologne took the opposite course and downright outlawed the making of bottom-fermented beers.

From 1607 onward, only city council ale was permitted to be poured in Cologne, and beer sales declined, as did revenues. Desperate for cash,

the city council soon reversed itself and leased the brew right back to the private brewers. As a result, the number of breweries increased again, to about ninety.

However, the place of kölsch as a German ale style had by then been firmly secured, though one feeble attempt at a lager takeover was made in Cologne in 1830, when the banking dynasty of the Rothschilds decided to pour substantial amounts of money into a large state-of-the-art brewery for bottom-fermented beer. The brew, however, turned out to be no good because the cellars lacked adequate cooling. The company soon failed and was converted to a sugar factory.

Alt—An Old Faithful

The beginnings of brewing in Düsseldorf are less well documented than those of Cologne. In Düsseldorf, as anywhere else in Germany, brewing had become the privilege of the monasteries by the ninth century. The convent at Gerresheim (now a suburb of Düsseldorf) was the first to be conferred the brewright, by Archbishop Wilhelm of Cologne in 873. In the convent's founding charter, the bishop insisted that the church devote more

resources to the production of quality beer. Soon six nunneries and monasteries in his diocese would enjoy the brewright. We know of another local convent that made unhopped beer around 1100. Records from the middle of the fourteenth century give evidence of a growing number of baker-brewers plying their trade, mostly in *Keutebier.*

The city's land-tax register from 1540–41 mentions the names of thirty-five brewers. The local duke, Wilhelm III, issued a police ordinance regulating the quality and price of beer served to the public. At the same time, beer from outside the city was heavily taxed to protect the local producers.

Beer became an ever more important matter of public policy. In 1622, the Düsseldorf bakers' and brewers' guild was constituted. As we know from the 1632 land-tax register, the house at Bergerstraße 1, the present-day home of the famous alt beer brewpub *Uerige* was then shared by Martin Pütz, a baker, and Diederich Pfeilsticker, an innkeeper. The founder of the present brewpub, Hubert Wilhelm Cürten, was also a baker with brewing credentials. He got his brewery license in 1855.

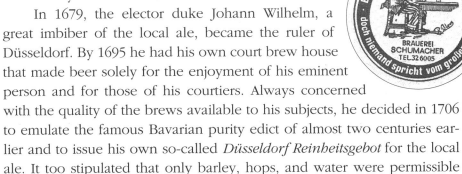

In 1679, the elector duke Johann Wilhelm, a great imbiber of the local ale, became the ruler of Düsseldorf. By 1695 he had his own court brew house that made beer solely for the enjoyment of his eminent person and for those of his courtiers. Always concerned with the quality of the brews available to his subjects, he decided in 1706 to emulate the famous Bavarian purity edict of almost two centuries earlier and to issue his own so-called *Düsseldorf Reinheitsgebot* for the local ale. It too stipulated that only barley, hops, and water were permissible as ingredients for the local brew. In 1709 a Düsseldorf police ordinance decreed that "nobody may tap a cask that is not at least several days old, is bright and well-sedimented" (Rümmler 1985).

To raise the standards of the Düsseldorf brewing craft further, in 1712 Johann Wilhelm licensed the first Düsseldorf guild for brewers only, ending the heretofore cozy union of bakers and brewers. Of course, this decision met with vociferous objections from the bakers, who lamented the loss of a separate source of income. The new guild started out with fifty-seven founding members. By 1768 it had grown to ninety-four members.

The year 1838 witnessed the opening of the oldest still operating alt beer brewpub in Düsseldorf, the *Brauerei Schumacher*. Its founder, Mathias Schumacher, took the traditional Rhineland ale as he found it but added a bit more hops than was customary at the time, brewed it stronger, and started to experiment with aging the beer in wooden casks to let it mature. In Schumacher's innovations lie the roots of the modern alt beer

style: a robust, coppery, slow-fermented, lagered ale. By 1871 Schumacher's operation, then under his son Ferdinand's management, had outgrown its original facilities. A new brewery was built at 129 Oststraße, where, happily for the modern connoisseur, the same alt is still brewed and served today.

Düsseldorf, the upstart cow town on the Rhine that received its city charter in 1288, eventually became a serious rival of Cologne in all facets of life that matter to Germans, from soccer to carnival to beer. Today, Düsseldorf is the capital of North Rhine–Westphalia, a renowned center of fashion and finance, and the home of Germany's most revered ale, the alt, that rich, mellow brew of unsurpassed elegance.

Other Alt Beers

Cities such as Oelde, Münster, and Steinfurt in Westphalia, Frankfurt in Hesse, Hannover in Lower Saxony, and even Großostheim, a small village near Aschaffenburg in Bavaria, make alt beers too, though these beers have been historically less significant in establishing the style. The brewers in these locales are obviously less finicky about naming their beers than are the brewers of Cologne. Like the Düsseldorfers, they call their brew "alt." Most of these alt beers are similar to the Düsseldorf model, with southern alt beers being a bit sweeter and maltier, Hannoverian alts slightly darker, and alts from Münster spicier because of the addition of up to 40% of wheat to the grain bill.

To become an accomplished alt drinker in Hannover, incidentally, you have to learn the custom of downing what is called in the local vernacular a *Lüttje Lage* (perhaps best translated as "little layer"). Hold a glass of clear, unflavored schnapps *and* an alt glass in *one* hand, with the alt glass between the thumb and first finger and the schnapps glass between the first and second fingers. Make sure that the rim of the schnapps glass is slightly higher than that of the beer glass. When you raise the alt glass to your lips, tilt it in such a way that the schnapps cascades into the beer, fortifying it as you drink.

Preserving the Past

Today, many kölsch breweries also make Pils style lagers, and some Düsseldorf alt breweries offer wheat ales. There is a tendency now, with corporate mergers and the formation of national beer conglomerates, to blur the geographic lines that once separated the different beer styles and their traditions. But credit is due to the Rhineland for preserving the three-thousand-year-old ale heritage as a still-vibrant expression of culture during a time when the global lager revolution turned most of the "old" brews into "beerological" fossils.

Weizen, the Bavarian Ale Holdover

Weizenbier (wheat beer) is another old-style brew that has seen its ups and downs. Wheat, like barley, had been a natural raw material of beer since the beginning of recorded history, if not earlier, but its use in Germany declined steadily during the last thousand years. At the turn of the twentieth century few breweries bothered with the style at all. Only during the last quarter century has wheat beer, including the turbid, unfiltered hefeweizen, seen a spectacular revival, especially among the young, and not only in its former stronghold of Bavaria. A surprising one out of every ten glasses of beer consumed in some parts of Germany nowadays is made from wheat.

Most German wheat-beer breweries are located in Bavaria and Baden-Würtemberg (Swabia), with the region around Munich accounting for the bulk of them. Wheat beer is always highly effervescent, and often somewhat sour. Its alcohol content is typically between 4.8% and 5.4% abv.

German law dictates that a wheat beer must contain at least 50% wheat. The rest is usually pale malt. This grain combination typically produces a beer that when filtered is called kristallweizen, a blonde, "crystal" clear beverage. When unfiltered and bottle-conditioned it is called hefeweizen because the yeast *(Hefe)* is still in suspension. The addition of dark barley or dark wheat malts to the grain bill results in deep copper to rust brown beers called dunkelweizen. Dunkelweizen is brewed

Wheat beer is spritzy and must be poured with patience.

mostly in eastern Bavaria, near the Czech border, where water is softer than in the area around Munich. Harder water would leach acrid substances out of the darker malts and give the beer a harsh finish. Likewise, harder water would enhance hop bitterness in a beer whose style is defined in part by low hoppiness. Like most Bavarian beers, a German wheat beer is also characterized by a rich maltiness, but unlike any other beer in Germany, it should be somewhat spicy, clovelike, and fruity. The fruitiness comes from the fermentation by-products generated by the ale yeast during an initial vigorous burst of fermentation at room temperature—an unusual technique in an area of Germany that has been known for its dedication to cold fermentation ever since the middle of the sixteenth century.

Weizenbock, like any bock, is a strong beer, available in Germany in both the hell and dunkel versions. Its alcohol content is generally about 6.5–7% abv.

For the record, and this may come as a surprise to North Americans, in Germany, wheat beers are rarely served with a lemon slice! Subjectively, most Germans consider the lemon flavor incompatible with the spiciness of a wheat ale. Objectively, they have learned that the lemon juice destroys the foamy head that is so typical of the effervescent weizen.

Berliner Wheat, a Spritzy, Sour Summer Refresher

Berliner weisse is a tart, low-alcohol wheat beer with about 2.5–3.5% abv and an extract rating of 7–8%, which puts it into the tax collector's classification of a *Schankbier* (draft beer), even though it is never served on tap because of its exceptional effervescence.

Nobody seems quite certain when Berliner weisse started. Some sources speculate that the beer originated in Bohemia and was brewed in Berlin as early 1572, whereas others insist that it became a local brew not before the 1680s. Traditionally, before glass beer bottles had come into use, Berliner weisse was sold in earthenware crocks closed with string-fastened cork stoppers to contain the beer's powerful carbonation. When Napoleon and his troops occupied Berlin in 1809, they dubbed it "the Champagne of the north." More-down-to-earth Berliners just called it the "the worker's sparkling wine" (Gerlach et al. 1984).

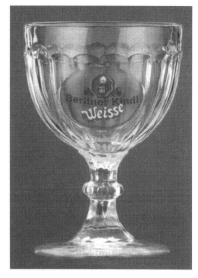

Berliner weisse is an extremely dry and effervescent beer with a decidedly sour taste. Low in hops flavor, it has a sharp acidic finish that stems from lactobacillus bacteria that are added with the ale yeast in the fermenter to produce lactic acid. Berlin's water is hard, which also contributes to the beer's astringency. The grain for Berliner weisse is between 60% and 75% wheat, the rest is pale Pils malt. Because of its tartness, Berliner weisse is usually consumed *mit Schuss,* "with a shot" of raspberry or woodruff-flavored syrup poured with the beer into a bowl-shaped glass.

A chilled Berliner weisse can be very refreshing, especially on a hot summer afternoon, when you might be sitting in an outdoor pub at the Kurfürstendamm, Berlin's showcase avenue, and watching the elegant passersby.

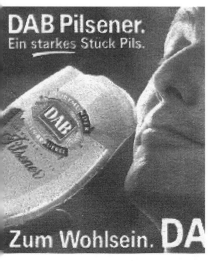

DAB Pilsener.
Ein starkes Stück Pils.

Zum Wohlsein. DA

chapter 13

German Lager Styles

■ ■ ■ ■ ■ ■ ■ ■ ■ ■ ■ ■ ■ ■ ■ ■ ■ ■ ■ ■

German lagers progress in color and flavor from very pale to very dark. All German lagers are Bavarian in origin except for the Bohemian Pilsner, the Westphalian Dortmunder export, the northern German Pils or Pilsener, and the Vienna lager. Even these four have some Bavarian lineage. The original Bohemian lager was designed by a Bavarian brewmaster, the Vienna lager under the influence of a Bavarian brewmaster, and the other two were express imitations of Bavarian models.

There is no doubt that the Bavarians are the world's lager pioneers. Helles, Märzen, Oktoberfest, bock, doppelbock, dunkel, schwarzbier, and rauchbier are all home-grown Bavarian. The Bavarians make lagers of any color and strength but not of all flavors. Bavarian-style beers tend to be low in hop bitterness and to have a rich, malty, sometimes even sweet finish that is never toasty or acrid, not even in the darkest of the dark lagers, the schwarzbier. Only the roasted, bacony-flavored rauchbier (which means "smoked beer" in German) is an exception to the rule.

Bavarian beers are always full-bodied, even when their color is the palest shade of golden blonde. Continental European barley has always been relatively high in proteins, which contribute body and mouthfeel to beer.

The color of Bavarian beers is directly related to the grains from which they are made. The workhorse of Bavarian brewing, in fact of German brewing in general, is the pale Pils malt *(helles Malz)*. It is a two-row summer barley that is allowed to germinate (malt) at or slightly below room temperature for up to seven days and is then dried gently for one to three days. The result of this rather slow drying cycle is a Pils malt that is quite pale by North American standards but is excellently suited for the golden blonde lagers of Germany.

Vienna malts *(Wiener Malz)* are a shade darker than Pils malts. They are made from the same barley but undergo a longer kilning regimen at slightly higher temperatures. The result is a slightly brownish but not roasted malt ideally suited for the amber to brown lagers of the Märzen, Vienna, and Oktoberfest styles.

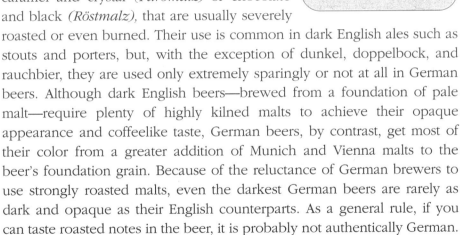

Munich malts (dark, *dunkel, Münchener Malz)* are darker yet. They are dried even longer and at a higher temperature. The result is a slightly roasted, but never burned, grain. As the name implies, the dark Munich lagers take their color mostly from Munich malts.

There are even darker malts, called caramel and crystal *(Farbmalz)* or chocolate and black *(Röstmalz),* that are usually severely roasted or even burned. Their use is common in dark English ales such as stouts and porters, but, with the exception of dunkel, doppelbock, and rauchbier, they are used only extremely sparingly or not at all in German beers. Although dark English beers—brewed from a foundation of pale malt—require plenty of highly kilned malts to achieve their opaque appearance and coffeelike taste, German beers, by contrast, get most of their color from a greater addition of Munich and Vienna malts to the beer's foundation grain. Because of the reluctance of German brewers to use strongly roasted malts, even the darkest German beers are rarely as dark and opaque as their English counterparts. As a general rule, if you can taste roasted notes in the beer, it is probably not authentically German.

Helles—Germany's Mainstay Brew

Helles (or helles export) is *the* staple beer of today's Bavarian drinker. It is also the beer most tourists know from the beer tents of the Munich Oktoberfest, where it has long since replaced the traditional strong Märzen or Oktoberfest beer as the generic crowd pleaser. Served in liter mugs, it is intended to be guzzled—though its alcoholic strength can be substantial, up to 5% abv.

Because the water in much of Bavaria is hard and carbonate—properties that would accentuate hops bitterness—hop loadings for helles are very minimal and of noble lineage only, mostly from Tettnang, Hallertau, and Spalt. This preserves the malty notes of the style. As a classic blonde German lager, helles is aged (lagered) near the freezing point for weeks after fermentation to bring out its delicacy and softness.

Bohemian Pilsner: The Mother of Modern Lagers

The western Bohemian city called Plzeň in Czech and Pilsen in German is the beneficiary of several uncanny natural advantages that put it smack in the center of the brew map of the world. Pilsen is located near the Zatec region (whose German name is Saaz), home of Saaz hops, the most fragrant and aromatic of the noble hops varieties.

Pilsen is also surrounded by fields of Hanna and Kniefl, the best two-row summer-brewing barley money can buy, and it is blessed with one of the world's softest waters. Thus, Pilsen had all the ingredients needed for a delicate, pale, aromatic beer. Only two elements were missing: a lager yeast—which a Bavarian monk brought to Pilsen in 1842—and a brewer familiar with cold fermentation—which the Pilsners found in Josef Groll, an emigrant Bavarian brewmaster from Vilshofen. With all the ingredients at hand, Groll made a radical departure from the brown, sweet brews of his era and created the golden Pilsen style in 1842. The soft water allowed for the brewing of a beer with a delicate, soft palate and a dry, hoppy finish. Groll's lager from Pilsen, called Pilsner (without the middle "e") was an instant sensation, enticing other Bohemian breweries to jump on the golden lager bandwagon. One such brewery was located in a town called Ceské Budéjovice in Czech and Budweis in German. The

By 1890, beer transport by rail had become big business, as shown here in a drawing of the Munich train station.

town's beer was called Budvar in Czech and Budweiser in German. Budweiser beers became popular with many royal houses in Europe and were thus known as "the beer of kings."

Beers from Pilsen and other Bohemian cities soon rumbled over the growing network of railways to the major centers of the Austro-Hungarian Empire and beyond. In Vienna it gave the local amber lager, introduced by the Dreher brewery a year earlier, a run for its money. In Paris, it became the *bière à la mode*.

Initially, Pilsner beers did not find favor with the average German drinker, though. Germans were used to something maltier and less hop-aromatic. Only in Berlin did Pilsner become a fad. By 1872, with the Franco-Prussian War over and Prussian power at its height, Pilsner was considered the most elegant drink in the imperial capital. Because Berlin then set the tone in all things political and fashionable in the reemerging Germany, Pilsner finally embarked on its conquest of the breweries and beer halls of Germany as well. In the cradle of European beers, the style became Pils, or Pilsener (with an "e" in the middle). It was brewed similarly to the Bohemian original but usually with an assertive rather than fragrant hoppiness.

To judge if a Pilsner is true to style, look for an aromatic hops finish rather than a malt finish (which would be characteristic of a Bavarian helles). Because of the soft water, this beer is rounded, not rough, in spite of the relatively high hop loading. The result is a very subtle balance in the finish. True Pilsners have between 4% and 5.5% abv. They are full-bodied and though not excessively carbonated have a long-lasting foamy head. On tap, it may take as much as seven minutes of repeated pouring to fill a glass.

If imitation is the most sincere form of flattery, the lager from Pilsen ranks tops on the scale of accolades. As a style it has been copied with some local modifications—but never equaled—in virtually every country in the world. Pilsners and their offshoots have since become the dominant beer style on the globe.

In the United States it was exactly the Bohemian golden lagers that Eberhard Anheuser tried to emulate when he purchased a small brewery in St. Louis, Missouri, in 1860. Joined by his son-in-law Augustus Busch a year later, he settled on a Budweiser version of the style, copied its name, and turned the original's slogan around, proclaiming his brew to be "the king of beers." Today, all major American breweries make mass-market "Pilsners," but these beers contain cheap barley substitutes—called adjuncts—such as rice and corn, which diminish the body and flavor of the brews. "Pilsners" made with adjuncts are simply misnomers.

Mouth-Puckering German Pils/Pilsener

German Pils is paler in color than Bohemian Pilsner and has a more definite up-front hoppiness and a much drier, hoppy finish. Whereas the brewers of the Czech Republic tend to use the aromatic Saaz for bittering, flavor, and aroma, German brewers prefer to use other noble hop varieties, such as Hallertau and Tettnang. Combined with the hard waters of the north, liberal doses of these hops produce a brew of lasting bitterness. The farther north the Pils is brewed, the more pungent and assertive is its hop profile. The driest, hoppiest examples of German Pils come from Friesland, right next to the Danish border.

Dortmunder Export—
Deep Golden and Balanced

The Westphalian city of Dortmund is in the center of the German coal and steel industry—not the sort of place you would associate with great beer—but Dortmund brews more beer nowadays than any other city in Europe. Strangely, the beer style to which the city gave its name is no longer among the popular ones produced by the city's breweries. Like most breweries in present-day Germany, the Dortmunders stress their Pilseners, the style that accounts for more than half of all German beer sales.

Jever Pils from the Frisian part of Lower Saxony, near the Danish border, is one of the driest and hoppiest German beers.

People have been brewing in Dortmund at least since 1266. The earliest Dortmunder brews were probably top-fermented wheat beers seasoned with *gruit*. After the lager revolution in Bavaria, Austria, and Bohemia in the 1840s, Dortmund was among the first northern cities to switch to bottom-fermenting yeast. By the 1870s, Dortmunder brewers had crafted their own golden blonde style of lager. Because of its early popularity in the northwestern part of Germany and in what are now Holland and Belgium, it was named *export*. In those days, the Germans often named a high-extract beer an export if it had enough keeping quality to be shipped overland or by sea. In the late nineteenth century Dortmunder became the leading beer in most parts of Germany until it gave way, after the First World War, to the helles style.

Brewed with fairly hard water, the flavor of Dortmunder export ranks somewhere between that of a Bohemian Pilsner, a northern German Pils, and a Bavarian helles. It is golden, with a solid hop flavor that is more definite than that of a helles, less fragrant than that of a Pilsner, and less puckering than that of a Pils. It is fairly malty, but drier

My mug foameth over.

than a helles. Today, it has about 4.5–5% abv, but in the old days its strength was probably closer to between 5% and 6% abv.

Vienna, Märzen, Oktoberfest

Next on the color scale is the deep golden to amber beer variably called Märzen, Vienna, or Oktoberfest. It has a very malty finish and subdued hop bitterness. Its alcoholic strength is typically around 4.5–5% abv. As its name implies, both Bavaria and Austria can lay claim to its origins. The beer is the result of a collaboration between two brewers, Gabriel Sedlmayr of Munich and Anton Dreher of Vienna. In 1833, both toured England's breweries to learn about the most recent advances in brewing there. They were especially impressed by British malting techniques, which gave brewers much paler malts than were available in Germany.

In the early nineteenth century the Austro-Hungarian Empire included, in addition to Austria and Hungary, Bohemia (now the western portion of the Czech Republic) and much of the Balkans. Austria was the undisputed political power in southern central Europe, and neighboring Bavaria was the undisputed beer power. The standard Bavarian brew of the early nineteenth century was a dark *(dunkel)* lager, strong, sweet, malty, and probably very turbid. It was made from well-kilned Munich malt.

The standard brew in the Austro-Hungarian Empire was virtually the same beer, only brewed with top-fermenting (ale) yeast. Dreher, however, switched to Sedlmayr's bottom-fermenting yeast and to barley from Moravia (now the eastern portion of the Czech Republic) that was less rigorously kilned. We now call such grains Vienna malt. Sedlmayr, on the other hand, stuck to his yeast but switched to Dreher's malt. The result was, in 1841, the introduction of the same new beer in both Vienna and Munich.

Brewed especially strong in March *(März)* and lagered in cool caves, where it could mature until being consumed during summer and early fall, the Vienna-style March beer soon took its place next to the traditional Munich dunkel and to that other new entry in the field of lagers, the Pilsner from Bohemia.

It did not take long before the Märzen began to replace the Munich dunkel as the favorite brew at the annual Munich Oktoberfest. Though Märzen had fallen out of favor with the public by the end of the First World War and been replaced by the lighter helles, its erstwhile role as the Oktoberfest beer has given it its most enduring designation. Bavarian breweries to this day affix the Oktoberfest name to their annual fall offerings of the style. The Vienna versions tend to be slightly less well aged and slightly lower in alcohol content, about 4.5% abv, whereas the Märzen/Oktoberfest versions typically have an alcohol content closer to 5% abv and require the entire six-month aging cycle to reach full maturity.

Bavarian Dunkel—The Original Lager

Dunkel ("dark" in German) is the traditional Bavarian lager. Until the 1820s the beer was dark by necessity because the direct-heat smoke kilns of the time were incapable of producing pale malt. Now, of course,

its color is chosen deliberately. Like all Bavarian beers, dunkel is predominantly malty in the finish without lacking in softness and elegance. Made mostly from Munich malts, the sweetness of dunkel is never cloying. The beer's hop character is typically Bavarian— that is, subdued. The up-front hops note comes from a mild bittering hops, such as Tettnang, followed by the lingering finish of a noble aroma hops, such as Saaz.

Schwarzbier— Looks Can Be Deceiving

Schwarzbier ("black beer") is the darkest of the dunkels, but not quite as dark as a stout. This beer is difficult to brew well, because the requirements for color and flavor seem to be contradictory. The schwarzbier grain bill is composed of large quantities of Munich malt with sparing additions of the more high-temperature-kilned color and roasted malts. The resulting maltiness may be spicy but must never be acrid. Though a dark beer, the clean lager taste must always be evident. If you drink a properly brewed schwarzbier with your eyes closed, you could swear it might be a dunkel or even a Märzen. It has none of the toastiness, fruity hoppiness, or sweetness we have come to associate with certain English-style dark ales. Instead, it has a very strong, but not cloyingly overpowering, malt aroma. The finish is surprisingly dry. The alcoholic strength of schwarzbier can vary greatly, from 4.5–5.5% abv.

Smoke Gets in My Grain—Rauchbier

Rauchbier is a dark lager and a specialty of the Franconian city of Bamberg in northern Bavaria. The smokiness, which imparts a bacony flavor to the beer, comes from beechwood logs that are used to fire the direct-heat kiln in which the malted grain is still dried today. This drying is similar to the kilning of malt over peat moss for Scotch whiskey. Perhaps an oddity in our day, smoke beer was probably quite common in the old days, when all malted barley was kiln-dried over wood fires. It would have been inevitable that the smoke would penetrate the moist layer of grain and impart its flavors, interesting or ugly, to the brewer's grist.

To many people, rauchbier is an acquired taste. It does go well with smoked cheeses, smoked pork chops, or smoked sausages. It is also wonderful for marinating a pork roast or for basting a suckling pig or leg of lamb over a barbecue. Rauchbier is brewed and aged similarly to an Oktoberfest beer, but the color is deeper, almost black, and there is usually a bit more hops in the brew to counter-balance the otherwise too assertive smokiness. The alcohol content of rauchbier is typically around 5.5% abv.

Bock—The Ale Turned Lager

Though Einbeck in Lower Saxony is the home of the original bock— some believe since about 1250—we now associate bock mostly with the city of Munich. The original bock was a strong brown ale, probably made with the addition of wheat. But by 1610 bock was "Bavarianized" by a brewmaster recruited from Einbeck and became a strong lager, similar to a Märzen but with a deeper, rich amber color. Bock beers are very malty indeed. In typical Bavarian fashion, they have very little but very noble hops notes for bitterness and flavor. Bocks must be fermented very cold and very slowly to achieve their mellow, malty quality. The best bock beers are aged (lagered) for several months. A younger bock would not be palatable, because its maltiness and alcohol would taste too raw and too obvious. Only when mellowed out is its 6–6.5% alcohol masked by mature sweetness. Be careful, though, this bock can kick!

The palest of the bocks is maibock, also known as helles bock, usually produced for the month of May. A darker and even stronger bock is doppelbock, the old "liquid bread" traditionally brewed by monks for the Lenten season. Doppelbock typically has an alcohol content of at least 6.8% abv, but 7.2% is not uncommon. The first commercial doppelbock was brewed by the Paulaner monks of Munich, who named it "Salvator," after their other passion in life, the Savior. This was in 1780. Since then, many doppelbocks feature the suffix "ator" in their name, for

instance, Maximator, Triumphator, or Celebrator. Doppelbock is by far Germany's "biggest" beer. The strongest of it, the eisbock, may have an alcohol content of as much as 9–11%. The really fat eisbocks are velvet hammers at about 16% abv.

Legend has it that eisbock was discovered by accident around 1890, when a tired brewery apprentice, at the end of a fourteen-hour shift, was too beat to move casks of fermented bock from the yard into the cellar, as he had been told to do. The night turned out to be bitter cold, and when the brewers returned the following morning, they found the casks of bock frozen, their wooden staves burst, and in the middle of each icy clump a bubble of brownish liquid.

The enraged brewmaster unwittingly meted out punishment of the most blissful kind. He ordered the hapless apprentice to chop open the frozen hunks of beer and drink the obviously unpalatable residue in the center, which, instead of stomach cramps, produced nothing but expressions of delight from the lad. The liquid was malty, sweet, and strong. It was eisbock. Because water freezes before alcohol and because the cold attacked the casks from the outside in, the center contained the essence of bock, with its malt flavors dissolved in alcohol. This legend may not be based on fact—we just don't know—but it is too good a yarn to pass up.

This EKU Kulminator Urtyp Hell 28 label proudly proclaims that the content of the bottle is *Das Stärkste Bier der Welt* (the strongest beer in the world). It is brewed in the northern Bavarian town of Kulmbach and weighs in at a hefty 28% extract for a substantial 13.5% alcohol by volume.

German Beer in History:
A Chronology

■ ■

Circa 2000 to 1500 B.C.

Germanic and Celtic tribal brewsters start making ale from wheat and barley in northern Europe.

Circa 800 B.C.

A German gentleman is buried with crocks of black beer, the first archaeological evidence of German beer making.

Circa 450 B.C.

The beer-hating Romans first encounter the beer-loving Germans.

A.D. 98

The Roman historian Tacitus ridicules German beer and German drinking habits in his works—the best preserved written records of early German beer culture.

Circa 450

Ale-drinking Germanic hordes plunder and pillage along the Apennine Peninsula, and the decaying Roman Empire collapses.

Circa 500

Hausfrau brewsters continue the German beer tradition in their tribal homes.

Circa 780

Charlemagne regulates brewing and starts estate breweries, and monks cultivate the first hops near Munich and start monastic breweries. This is the beginning of professional large-scale brewing in Germany.

Circa 900

The Catholic Church secures a virtual beer monopoly from the feudal lords.

924

King Henry I of Germany coins the word "burgher" and with it identifies a new social class that will ultimately challenge the brew monopoly of the nobles and the clergy.

962

The First German *Reich* (empire) is founded by Otto I.

Circa 1000

Brewmonks and brewnuns make great ales and get very rich on them.

Circa 1200

Feudal lords build court breweries *(Hofbräuhäuser),* mostly in the south, to spite the monks, and burghers build private city breweries mostly in the north, to spite both. As a result, Bavarian beers take a turn for the worse, despite regulation, while northern beers take a turn for the better.

Circa 1250

The Hanseatic League starts a trading empire for northern German ales. The rigid horse collar and the iron horseshoe make overland beer transport possible. The city of Einbeck starts making an ale-style bock beer.

1288

The Battle of Worringen and the founding of Düsseldorf lay the foundations for the future development of alt beer, Germany's copper-colored traditional ale.

1438

The founding of Cologne's brewers' guild places the brewing of the local ale, a forerunner of today's kölsch, firmly in the hands of free-enterprise-loving burghers.

1516

The Bavarian beer purity law *(Reinheitsgebot)* is proclaimed. It is the oldest food quality law in Germany—and perhaps the world. It stipulates that only barley, water, and hops may be used in beer making.

1517

Luther nails his Ninety-Five Theses to the door of the castle church at Wittenberg and starts the Reformation. Beer from Einbeck sustains him.

1526

The 531 breweries in Hamburg employ half the city's population.

1553

Summer brewing is outlawed in Bavaria. As a result of brewing only in winter, Bavarians start making lagers without knowing it.

1566

The ducal Bavarian House of Wittelsbach outlaws wheat-beer making to curb the revenues from the wheat-beer monopoly enjoyed by the House of Degenberg and to secure a popular market for the new lagers made according to the *Reinheitsgebot*.

1572

By some accounts, Berlin brewers start to make an effervescent, very dry wheat ale. Supposedly an adaptation of a Bohemian brew, they call theirs Berliner weisse. (Other chroniclers date the beginning of the Berliner brew a century later, to the 1680s.)

1589–1590

Duke Wilhelm V of Bavaria, grandson of the *Reinheitsgebot* duke Wilhelm IV, builds the first *Hofbräuhaus* in Munich, on the site of the present *Hofbräuhaus*. He dedicates it to the exclusive brewing of a brown *Reinheitsgebot* lager, the forerunner of all modern Bavarian lagers.

1602

The line of Degenbergers dies out, the wheat-beer monopoly reverts to the House of Wittelsbach, and wheat beer becomes legal again in Bavaria. Duke Maximilian I, great-grandson of the *Reinheitsgebot* duke Wilhelm IV, builds a second *Hofbräuhaus* in Munich for wheat beer only next to the existing brown-lager brewery.

1603

Lager brewing is outlawed in Cologne to defend the local kölsch ale against a wave of lager brewing spreading north from southern Germany.

1606

Libavius theorizes that there is a difference between fermentation and putrefaction. He thus opens the door to the scientific study of fermentation.

1612

Bock beer, a lager copy of the original Einbeck ale, as well as wheat beer conquer Bavaria. The two beers are supported by edicts from the House of Wittelsbach to secure the ducal markets and—burdened by taxes—to secure the ducal riches.

1618

Start of the Thirty Years' War, which ruins the northern German brew industry and causes the collapse of the merchant beer-trading empire there. As a result, northern beer making stagnates while Bavarian lager-beer making takes the lead in quality and innovation. Only in the Rhineland do traditional German ales develop into distinct styles that survive to the present as Düsseldorf alt and Cologne kölsch.

1674

Van Leeuwenhoek discovers the existence of yeast.

1706

Proclamation of the Düsseldorf beer purity law ensures the integrity and purity of ales from the Rhineland.

1780

The first commercial doppelbock is brewed by the Paulaner monks of Munich, who name it Salvator.

1789

Lavoisier discovers that carbon dioxide and ethanol are products of alcoholic fermentation. The French Revolution spawns the liberalization of all facets of society in most of Europe, including the brew laws in Germany.

1791

The French abolish occupational guilds. This puts an end to German brewers' guilds as the French army rolls over Europe.

1803

Beer-selling monopolies are abolished in French-occupied northern Germany.

1806

The First German Empire ceases to exist after the last incumbent abdicates the throne in the face of rising French power in Europe. More than eight centuries of German political and brewing history come to an end. Beer-selling monopolies are abolished in Bavaria.

1809

The French army under Napoleon occupies Berlin. They encounter the bubbly Berliner weisse wheat ale and dub it the "Champagne of the north."

1810

First Munich Oktoberfest on the occasion of the marriage between the Bavarian crown prince Ludwig I and Princess Therese of Sachsen-Hildburghausen.

1818

Invention of the hot-air kiln, which is fired by indirect heat. This makes the production of pale malts and of pale beers possible.

1837

Schwann discovers that yeast is a living organism and that the fermentation of sugars into alcohol is an anaerobic process.

1841

Vienna brewer Anton Dreher and Munich brewer Gabriel Sedlmayr introduce a Vienna, or Märzen lager, which later becomes known as Oktoberfest beer.

1842

An immigrant brewer from Bavaria creates the first Pilsner Urquell in Bohemia, the first successful blonde lager and the mother of all modern lagers.

1843

Balling invents the hydrometer, which allows brewers to measure the extract strength of beer and thus make a more consistent product.

Circa 1850

Steam-heated brew kettles and mash tuns make their appearance first in Bavaria, then in the rest of Germany.

1860

German immigrant Eberhard Anheuser starts a small brewery in St. Louis, Missouri, which, in due course, becomes the biggest brewery in the world. Its flagship product, Budweiser, is an imitation of a Bohemian lager.

1868

Pasteur publishes his *Études sur la bière,* in which he explains the reproduction and metabolism of yeast. He also explains how bacteria can spoil beer unless they are killed by heat (pasteurization).

1871

Bismarck founds the Second German Empire under Prussian leadership. Beer taxes and beer quality standards are part of the legal code of the new empire. The Spaten Brewery introduces the Vienna/Märzen lager to the Oktoberfest in Munich, and the beer acquires its new name of *Oktoberfestbier.*

1872

The Bavarian House of Wittelsbach sells the wheat beer privilege to a private brewing company and thus end two and a half centuries of royal production monopolies in wheat beers.

1873

Linde invents refrigeration. Munich brewmaster Sedlmayr of the Spaten Brewery is the first to use it. Lagers can now be made anywhere, regardless of climate. Subsequently, lager beers sweep Europe (except for the Rhineland, Belgium, Holland, and the British Isles).

1878

Enzinger invents the beer filter.

1880

The number of German breweries reaches its peak of nineteen thousand. (Today, there are about twelve hundred.)

1881

Hansen isolates ale and lager yeast strains for the first time. Now brewers can work with pure yeast strains and make beers with predictable characteristics.

1890

O'Sullivan explains how enzymes convert unfermentable starches into fermentable sugars, and the mashing process is demystified. That same year, according to legend, eisbock is discovered by accident, when a brewery apprentice leaves several casks of fermented bock to freeze overnight.

1894

The Spaten Brewery makes the first blonde, clear, golden lager in Bavaria, a forerunner of the helles that ended the dominance of the traditional Bavarian brown lagers.

Circa 1900

Germany has become an international beer power. Every fourth glass of beer consumed in the world is made in Germany.

1906

The *Reinheitsgebot* becomes the official law in all the realm of the Kaiser.

1919

The end of the Second German Empire after the devastation of the First World War. The beginning of Germany's first attempt at democracy, the Weimar Republic, with its idealistic yet unworkable constitution, is formed.

1928

The Paulaner Brewery of Munich makes a helles that helps launch the blonde quaffing lager of Bavaria as the most popular beer style in Germany.

1933

The end of the Weimar Republic and the beginning of the Third German Empire, the Third *Reich*.

1945

The end of the Second World War and of the Third *Reich*.

1949

Germany's second attempt at a democratic republic, the still-existing Federal Republic.

Circa 1960

The hoppy, dry north German Pils takes almost 60% of the German beer market.

Circa 1980

With the resurgence in popularity of wheat beers from Bavaria, and of alt and kölsch from the Rhineland, ales rebound in the German marketplace and reach a combined share of almost one-fifth in some regions.

1987

The European Court strikes down the German *Reinheitsgebot* as an obstacle to free trade, although German brewers and drinkers continue to adhere to it to this day.

In the 1990s

Brewery mergers and closings as well as national beer conglomerates occur in the face of growing competition and declining beer consumption in Germany, but small brewpubs increase in numbers and popularity.

Glossary

■ ■

Abv. Abbreviation of "alcohol by volume." See *Alcohol*.

Abw. Abbreviation of "alcohol by weight." See *Alcohol*.

Adjuncts. Any unmalted cereal, such as rice or corn, and other fermentables added to beer as a starch substitute for malted barley or malted wheat. Adjuncts violate the *Reinheitsgebot* and are generally not used in German beers. In certain parts of Germany some brewers add sugar (often unfermentable), caramelized sugar (so-called *Zuckerkulör*), or saccharin to top-fermented beers, primarily as coloring agents. Such additions are always indicated on the label. Many of the low-alcohol *Malzbiers,* for instance, derive much of their sweetness and dark color from *Zuckerkulör*.

Aeration. The process by which sterile air (or pure oxygen) is pumped through fresh wort that is inoculated with yeast to stimulate the yeast's reproductive cycle. See *Pitching* and *Yeast*.

Aerobic. Life processes that require oxygen. Yeast has two phases of life, aerobic and anaerobic. In the presence of oxygen, yeast cells multiply. In the absence of oxygen, they ferment (that is, metabolize) sugars into alcohol, carbon dioxide, and other trace elements.

Alcohol. A product of fermentation. The type of alcohol produced by yeast varies with yeast strain, yeast health, fermentation temperature, and fermentation method. The desired alcohol in beer is ethanol. So-called higher alcohols have a higher boiling point than ethanol and can leave a "fusel" flavor in the beer. Alcohol is measured by weight (abw) or by volume (abv). Abv is the volume of alcohol as a percentage of the volume of beer in which it is in solution. Abw is the weight of alcohol as a percentage of the weight of the beer in which it is in solution. The abw figure is roughly 20% lower than the abv figure for the same beer, because a given amount of alcohol weighs less than the equivalent amount of water.

Ale. Any beer that is fermented with a strain of *Saccharomyces cerevisiae*. These are so-called top-fermenting yeasts that work best at temperatures between approximately 60–75 °F (16—24 °C).

Alpha acids. A type of hop resin that undergoes a change in its molecular structure (see *Isomerization*) when it is boiled in the wort. The resulting compounds, iso-alpha-acids, give the beer its up-front bitterness.

Amylase. A group of enzymes that reside naturally in the grain and convert unfermentable grain starches into fermentable and unfermentable sugars (see *Diastatic enzymes*). The most important of these enzymes are alpha-amylase and beta-amylase. Alpha-amylase are enzymes that specialize in producing complex sugars called dextrins, that are generally not fermentable by the yeast. Beta-amylase are enzymes that specialize in producing maltose (the most important fermentable sugar in beer) from starches and in the reduction of complex sugars into simple sugars.

Anaerobic. Life processes that occur in the absence of oxygen.

Attenuation. A quantitative measurement of the reduction of the specific gravity of wort as a result of fermentation. Prior to fermentation, a particular wort might have 12% extract. As fermentation progresses, more and more sugars are converted into alcohol and carbon dioxide. As a result, the wort gets "lighter," or more attenuated, until fermentation stops and the wort has a residual extract of, perhaps, 3–4%. At this point the beer is fully attenuated.

Barrel. In brewing, a U.S. barrel holds 31 U.S. gallons (1.17 hectoliters), whereas a British barrel holds 36 imperial gallons (1.63 hectoliters).

Beer. Any alcoholic undistilled drink made mostly from grain. Its main subcategories are ale and lager.

Biersteuergesetz. The German beer tax law, which regulates not only the tax rate paid by brewers but also the ingredients and processes permitted in malting grain and brewing beer.

Bierzwang. Literally, "beer coercion," the practice by medieval German municipalities of allowing only beer brewed (and taxed) in their jurisdictions to be served there. It was abolished and replaced by *Bierfreiheit* (literally, "beer freedom") in the early nineteenth century.

Brewster. A female brewer. Until the early Middle Ages, all beer in Germany was made by brewsters.

Carbonates. Alkaline salts whose negative ions are derived from carbonic acid.

Carbonation. The amount of carbon dioxide gas (CO_2) dissolved in finished beer. The more carbon dioxide is in the beer, the more effervescent it is. Excessive carbonation produces a "burpy," gassy beer. Too little carbonation produces a flat, pallid beer. Carbon dioxide is a natural byproduct of the yeast's fermentation. In a normal wort, the yeast produces more carbon dioxide than is needed for the finished beer. At the beginning of fermentation, therefore, carbon dioxide is allowed to escape the fermenter. At the end of fermentation, brewers often "cap" (that is, close) the fermenter to develop pressure in the beer tank and keep the remaining carbon dioxide dissolved in the beer. Before bottling or kegging beer, brewers usually correct its carbon dioxide content to the proper level by either bleeding off any excess or injecting additional amounts under pressure.

Carbon dioxide (CO_2). A gas composed of carbon and oxygen. Next to alcohol, carbon dioxide is the most important product of yeast fermentation. See *Carbonation*.

Cerevisia. Latin word for beer. Still used in scientific name for ale yeast, *Saccharomyces cerevisiae.*

Chicha. A beer made from corn by Peruvian Indians.

Chill haze. Cloudiness in beer caused by suspended proteins and tannins. The breakup of large proteins into small proteins by proteolytic enzymes is designed to reduce or eliminate chill hazes from protein. Careful timing of the length of sparging can prevent the excessive leaching of tannins from the grain and thus reduce chill hazes from this source. A good rolling boil in the brew kettle also helps to reduce chill hazes by coagulating proteins and colloiding tannins with proteins so that both may separate from the wort. Gums and cellulose are grain carbohydrates that can increase wort viscosity and form hazes in the beer unless they are properly degraded by enzymatic action in the mash tun. Regardless of the source of hazes, sharp filtration after fermentation can eliminate them before the beer reaches the consumer.

Decoction. The process by which part of the mash is removed, heated in a cooker, and then returned to the main mash to raise its temperature. Decoction aids in enzymatic action and the conversion of starches into sugars in poorly modified grains. See *Modification*.

Diastatic enzymes. Starch-converting substances in the grain that work as catalysts. They cause a chemical reaction in starch molecules without being themselves part of the resulting new compounds—sugars. The most important function of mashing is the activation of diastatic enzymes.

Dunkel. German word for "dark." Usually refers to a dark Bavarian lager.

Einfachbier. Literally, "simple beer." A German term for beers of low strength. Most nonalcoholic or low-alcohol beers fall into this category.

Emmer. A speltlike wheat used by the ancient Sumerians some four thousand years ago to make beer.

Enzymes. Protein-based organic substances that cause chemical changes in the substances upon which they act. See *Diastatic enzymes* and *Proteolytic enzymes*.

Esters. Aromatic compounds created through the interaction of organic acids with alcohols. In beer, they are created by enzymes in the yeast during fermentation and are often responsible for fruitiness or a bananalike flavor in the finished beer. Different yeast strains have different propensities for ester production. Ester production generally also increases with increased fermentation temperatures. Esters can be detected in low concentrations and are, to some extent, acceptable in certain ales but generally not in lagers.

Ethanol. The standard and most abundant form of alcohol produced by brewer's yeast under normal conditions.

Extract. The sugar-containing runoff from the mash tun. Extract also contains proteins, minerals, vitamins, flavor substances, and other trace elements from the grain. Its strength is measured as a percentage of dissolved substances (that is, everything other than water) in the runoff.

Fermentation. The process by which yeast converts sugars into alcohol and carbon dioxide.

Flocculation. The process by which yeast cells aggregate as sediment in the bottom of the tank after fermentation.

Grist. Milled or cracked grain before it is placed in the mash tun.

Gruit. Old German for "wild herbs," usually yarrow, bog myrtle, or juniper. Used to flavor beer until the early Middle Ages, before hops came into wide use. The term *gruit* eventually became synonymous with the tax every medieval German household had to pay to the authorities in exchange for the right to collect herbs and brew beer.

Head. The foamy white layer on top of the brew after it is poured into a glass. The head is made up mostly of proteins, dextrins (see *Sugars*), and carbon dioxide. A good head is considered essential in a quality German-style beer.

Hell (belles). German for "light" (in color only!). Usually a blonde lager.

Hofbräuhaus. A feudal court brew house, usually associated with a pub. In the old days, a great source of revenue for monopoly-minded overlords.

Hops. A clinging vine whose female flowers are used to give beer bitterness, flavor, and aroma.

Hydrolysis. The process by which substances (such as starches) are made water soluble. This occurs in mashing, when starches are hydrolyzed to make them accessible to enzymes, which convert starches to sugars.

Infusion. The process by which grain is "infused" with hot water during mashing. During step-infusion, the grain bed is infused twice or several times with water of different temperatures. The object is usually to activate proteolytic enzymes first and diastatic enzymes last. Proteolytic enzymes work best at a lower temperature range than do diastatic enzymes.

Isomerization. A process by which an organic compound changes its molecular structure but not its weight and composition. Under the influence of a vigorous boil, the alpha acids extracted from the hops change to iso-alpha-acids, which account for most of the bitterness in beer. See *Alpha acids* and *Hops*.

Kash. Old Egyptian word for beer. Kash was used as a currency to pay slaves and priests alike. It is the root of the modern English word "cash."

Keutebier. A medieval hopped wheat beer made mostly in northern Germany.

Kilning. The process of drying the grain after malting. The longer the kilning time and the higher the kilning temperature, the darker is the resulting brewing grain (and finished beer) and the lower is the number of enzymes that can be reactivated in the mash tun. Highly kilned malt must always be mixed in the mash tun with enzyme-rich pale malt to have a sufficient concentration of enzymes for diastatic and proteolytic conversion. See *Diastatic enzymes* and *Proteolytic enzymes*.

Lager. From the German verb *lagern*, "to store." Any beer fermented with strains of *Saccharomyces uvarum* (see *Yeast*), which work best at temperatures around 50 °F (10 °C). After fermentation, lagers are aged, or cold-conditioned, for several weeks to several months. Lagering near the freezing point helps to precipitate yeast and proteins and generally mellows the beer's taste.

Lautering. From the German verb *läutern*, "to clear or clarify." The process of draining the sugar-rich extract from the grain bed in the mash tun.

Malt. Grain that has been malted. See *Kilning* and *Malting*.

Malting. The process of steeping grain and allowing it to partially germinate. Germination is terminated by kiln-drying the grain. During malting, a portion of the grain's enzymes are activated. During the mashing of the grain in the brew house, the activation of the grain's enzymes continues.

Malz. German word for "malt."

Mashing. The process of steeping grain in hot water in the mash tun to hydrolyze (see *Hydrolysis)* carbon-based and nitrogen-based substances, degrade haze-forming proteins (see *Proteolytic enzymes)* and convert starches into sugars (see *Diastatic enzymes* and *Sugars).*

Maß. Originally a measure for a brewmonk's daily beer rations. Now a 1-liter beer mug.

Modification. A process that occurs during malting. It is a measure of the degree to which grain proteins have become soluble in water as a result of enzymatic action.

Oktoberfest. Originally a beerless public celebration of the wedding anniversary of the Bavarian Royal couple. The fest started in 1810. Today it is the biggest drinking party in the world and still held at the same place in Munich every year.

Pasteurization. Heating packaged beer or any food product to 140–175 °F (60–80 °C) for at least twenty minutes to make it microbiologically stable and extend its shelf life.

pH. Abbreviation of "potential hydrogen." It expresses the degree of acidity or alkalinity of a solution on a scale of 1 to 14 whereby 1 is extremely acidic, 7 is neutral, and 14 is extremely alkaline. Diastatic enzymes generally work best at a mash pH of roughly 5 to 5.5.

Phenols. Aromatic building blocks of polyphenols and tannins, which can contribute to stale or medicinal flavors in beer and to chill hazes.

Pitching. The process of introducing yeast, usually drawn in a thick slurry from a previously fermented batch, into fresh wort.

Protein rest. The time required during mashing for proteolytic enzymes to become active and convert large-molecule proteins into small-molecule proteins.

Proteins. Organic compounds whose basic building blocks are amino acids (formed from nitrogen) and carbon skeletons. The degradation of proteins during kilning and mashing frees amino acids. These are important as yeast nutrients. They affect yeast health and metabolism and thus the flavor and quality of the finished beer. See *Yeast.*

Proteolytic enzymes. Protein-converting substances in the grain that work as catalysts. They cause a chemical change in protein molecules, called *proteolysis,* without being themselves part of the resulting new compounds. During proteolysis in the mash tun, these specialized enzymes convert large proteins in the grain into small proteins. They also produce amino acids that are required for healthy yeast cultures. Small proteins are less likely to coagulate and separate in the brew kettle or get trapped in the beer filter. To the extent that they reach the finished beer, they contribute to its body and head.

Racking. The process of transferring wort or beer from one tank to another or into kegs.

Reinheitsgebot. The German beer purity decree first issued in Bavaria in 1516. It stipulated that only barley, hops, and water could be used in beer making. The function of yeast in fermentation was not known at that time. Since then, the *Reinheitsgebot* has been amended. It now insists that all barley used be "malted." It also allows for malted wheat in wheat ales and includes yeast as a beer-making ingredient.

Rest. Holding the mash at a specific temperature for a specific time to induce enzymatic reactions.

Saccharification. The process by which malt starch is converted into sugars, mostly maltose.

Schankbier. Literally, "draft beer." A German term for very light beers in any package.

Sparging. The process of sprinkling hot water over the grain bed during lautering until all the sugars are extracted from the grain.

Starkbier. Literally, "strong beer." A German term for very heavy beers, such as doppelbock.

Sugars. Also known as *saccharides,* sugars are by far the most important brewing hydrocarbons derived from the grain. Sugars are classified by their molecular complexity. Sugars with one to three molecules are generally fermentable by brewer's yeast, whereas sugars with four or more molecules generally are not. Fermentable saccharides are the source of alcohol and carbon dioxide in beer, and unfermentable saccharides stay in the finished beer as residual sugars and contribute to the beer's body, mouthfeel, and head. "Dry" or "light" beers are those without residual sugars. *Monosaccharides* are single-molecule sugars such as glucose and fructose. *Disaccharides* are two-molecule sugars such as maltose, sucrose (common table sugar, composed of one glucose and one fructose molecule), and melibiose. *Trisaccharides* are three-molecule sugars such as maltotriose and raffinose (a minor but important wort sugar composed of two melibiose molecules and one fructose molecule). *Oligosaccharides* are sugars of four or more molecules (complex sugars). *Polysaccharides* are complex sugars that are capable of being reduced to fermentable monosaccharides, and dextrins are polysaccharide fractions that cannot be reduced to fermentable saccharides. As a rule of thumb, the percentage of the most important sugars in wort is as follows: fructose 1–2%, sucrose 4–8%, glucose 8–10%, maltotriose 12–18%, maltose 46–50%. Ale yeasts *(Saccharomyces cerevisiae)* can ferment all sugars with one to three molecules, except for the melibiose portion of raffinose, whereas lager yeasts *(Saccharomyces uvarum)* can ferment melibiose molecules as well.

So-called wild yeasts, which create undesirable off-flavors in beer, are superattenuators (see *Attenuation*) that can ferment even dextrins.

Sugar rest. The time required during mashing for diastatic enzymes to become active and convert starches into sugars.

Tannins. Astringent phenolic substances in the grain and hops. If present in excess, tannins may impart a medicinal flavor to the finished beer.

Trub. The sediment of coagulated proteins, hop resins, polyphenols, vegetable gums, hop fibers, and other debris that accumulates at the bottom of the brew kettle during the boiling of the wort.

Vollbier. Literally, "whole beer." A German term for beers of medium strength. Ninety-nine percent of all German beers fall into this category.

Water hardness. General hardness is a measure of calcium and manganese ions dissolved in the water. Carbonate hardness is a more specific measure of carbonates dissolved in the water.

Wort. The sweet extract that is boiled in the brew kettle and, after the addition of hops, becomes unfermented beer.

Yeast. The Latin name for yeast, *Saccharomyces,* means "sugar fungus." In the scheme of biological classification, this sugar fungus belongs to the category of protists. These are single-celled organisms that scientists have not been able to anchor firmly into either the plant or the animal kingdom. They rank somewhere in between. Both yeasts and bacteria belong here. Yeasts, including the brewer's yeasts *Saccharomyces cerevisiae* and *Saccharomyces uvarum,* are protists of higher order, which scientists call eukaryotes. They are distinguished by the presence of cell nuclei and the ability to reproduce by cell division. Other eukaryotes are green algae, fungi, and protozoans (single-cell organisms). Bacteria, by comparison, which are spoilage organisms, belong in the category of prokaryotes. These are protists of lower order that lack true cell nuclei. For the brewer, *Saccharomyces* has two important life cycles: a reproductive phase and a metabolic phase. Under aerobic conditions, yeast reproduces itself vigorously through cell division. Under anaerobic conditions, yeast "eats," or metabolizes, sugars—a process we call fermentation. After fermentation yeast goes dormant until it is reintroduced to fresh wort with new sugar (see *Pitching*) to start the cycle again.

References and
Further Reading

■■■■■■■■■■■■■■■■■■■■■■■■■■■■■■■

Bishop, Morris. *Middle Ages*. Boston: Houghton Mifflin, 1987.

Bloch, Marc. *Feudal Society*. Vols. 1 and 2. London: Routledge & Kegan, 1991.

Brauerei Schumacher 1838–1988. Düsseldorf, 1988. A pamphlet published by the Schumacher Brauerei on the occasion of the brewery's 150th anniversary in September 1988.

Bridgwater, William, and Elizabeth Sherwood, eds. *The Columbia Encyclopedia*. 2nd ed. New York: Columbia University Press, 1950.

Burch, Byron. "Of Yeast and Beer Styles." *Zymurgy* 12, no. 4 (Special 1989).

Busch, Ernst. *Vom Beginn der Französischen Revolution 1789 bis zur Gegenwart*. 12th ed. Frankfurt: Diesterweg, 1965.

Butcher, Alan D. *Ale & Beer: A Curious History*. Toronto: McClelland & Steward, 1989.

Chapter of the Cathedral of Aachen. *The Treasury of the Cathedral of Aachen*. Aachen, Germany: 1986.

Daniels, Ray. *Designing Great Beers*. Boulder, Colo.: Brewers Publications, 1996.

Davies, Norman. *Europe: A History*. New York: Oxford University Press, 1996.

Eames, Alan. *Secret Life of Beer*. Pownal, Vt.: Storey Communications, 1995.

Eckhardt, Fred. *The Essentials of Beer Style*. Portland, Ore.: Fred Eckhardt Communications, 1989.

———. "The Hybrid Styles: Some Notes on Their Fermentation and Formulation." *Zymurgy* 12, no. 4 (Special 1989).

————. "German Style Ale." *Zymurgy* 14, no. 4 (Special 1991).

————. "Beer Traditions of Old Germany." *Zymurgy* 16, no. 4 (Special 1993).

Eden, Karl. "History of German Brewing." *Zymurgy* 16, no. 4 (Special 1993).

————. "History of German Oktoberfest." *Zymurgy* 16, no. 4 (Special 1993).

Ehrenfels-Mehringen, Erich von. *Gambrinus.* Duisburg, Germany: Carl Lange, 1953.

Fix, George. *Principles of Brewing Science.* Boulder, Colo.: Brewers Publications, 1989.

Fix, George, and Laurie Fix. *Oktoberfest, Vienna, Märzen.* Classic Beer Style Series, no. 4. Boulder, Colo.: Brewers Publications, 1991.

Foster, Terry. *Pale Ale.* Classic Beer Style Series, no. 1. Boulder, Colo.: Brewers Publications, 1990.

————. *Porter.* Classic Beer Style Series, no. 5. Boulder, Colo.: Brewers Publications, 1992.

Frane, Jeff. "Modern Altbier Demands Old Techniques." *Brew Your Own* 2, no. 10 (October 1996).

Friedrich, Ernst. *Bier.* Künzelsau, Germany: Sigloch, 1993.

Funke, Pia-Maria, Karl-Peter Fürst, Dr. Jörg Meidenbauer, Hanspeter Weigl. *Die schönsten Biergärten Deutschlands.* Munich, Stuttgart, Germany: RV Reise- und Verkehrsverlag GmbH, 1997.

Garetz, Mark. *Using Hops.* Danville, Calif.: Hop Tech, 1994.

Gerlach, Wolfgang, Hermann Gutmann, Michael Hassenkamp, Udo Moll, and Werner Widmann. *Das deutsche Bier.* Hamburg: HB Verlags- und Vertriebsgesellschaft, 1984.

Gesellschaft für Öffentlichkeitsarbeit der Deutschen Brauwirtschaft e.V., ed. *Vom Halm zum Glas.* Bonn: Gesellschaft für Öffentlichkeitsarbeit der Deutschen Brauwirtschaft, n.d.

Gold, Elizabeth, ed. *Evaluating Beer.* Boulder, Colo.: Brewers Publications, 1993.

Hans Sion-Stiftung, ed. *Kölner Brauhauswanderweg*. 2nd ed. Cologne: Bachem, 1995.

Hellex, Rolf. *Bier im Wort*. Nürnberg: Carl, 1981.

Heyse, Karl-Ulrich. *Handbuch der Brauereipraxis*. 3rd ed. Nürnberg: Carl, 1994.

Hillman, Howard. *The Gourmet Guide to Beer*. New York: Washington Square Press, 1983.

Jackson, Michael. *The New World Guide to Beer*. Philadelphia: Running Press, 1988.

———. *Michael Jackson's Beer Companion*. Philadelphia: Running Press, 1993.

———. *The Simon and Schuster Pocket Guide to Beer*. New York: Simon and Schuster, 1994.

Jung, Herrmann. *Bier—Kunst und Brauchtum*. Dortmund-Wichlinghofen, Germany: Documenta-Verlag Eugen Schinker, 1966.

Kaiser, A. "Praktische Hinweise zur Erzeugung von Altbieren." *Brauwelt* 118, no. 33 (August 1978).

Kieninger, H. "Altbiere." *Brauwelt* 120, no. 22 (May 1980).

King, Frank. *Beer Has a History*. London: Hutchinson's Scientific and Technical Publications, 1947.

Knoflicek, Zdenek, Jana Koutna, and Petr Zizkovsky. *Pivovarske Muzeum V Plzni*. Pilsen, Czech Republic: Pilsen Brewery, n.d.

Koehler, Wolfram. "Lager Beer—A Brief History." *Zymurgy* 16, no. 4 (Special 1993).

La Pensée, Clive. *The Historical Companion to House-Brewing*. Beverly, England: Montag Publications, 1990.

Lewis, Gregory. "Kiss of Hops." *The New Brewer* 11, no. 4 (August 1994).

Lewis, Michael. *Stout*. Classic Beer Style Series, no. 10. Boulder, Colo.: Brewers Publications, 1995.

Lohberg, Rolf. *Das große Lexikon vom Bier*. Ostfildern, Germany: Scripta, n.d.

Maronde, Curt. *Rund um das Bier.* Stuttgart: Steingrüben, 1969.

Mathar, Franz, and Rudolf Spiegel. *Kölsche Bier- und Brauhäuser.* Cologne: Greven, 1989.

Miller, David. *Continental Pilsener.* Classic Beer Style Series, no. 2. Boulder, Colo.: Brewers Publications, 1989.

Müller, Kristiane, ed. *Düsseldorf.* Hong Kong: APA Publications, 1991.

Narziß, Ludwig. *Die Technologie der Malzbereitung.* 6th ed. Stuttgart: Enke, 1976.

———. *Abriss der Bierbrauerei.* 5th ed. Stuttgart: Enke, 1986.

———. *Die Technologie der Würzebereitung.* 7th ed. Stuttgart: Enke, 1992.

Noonan, Gregory. *Brewing Lager Beer.* Boulder, Colo.: Brewers Publications, 1986.

———. *Scotch Ale.* Classic Beer Style Series, no. 8. Boulder, Colo.: Brewers Publications, 1994.

———. *New Brewing Lager Beer.* Boulder, Colo.: Brewers Publications, 1996.

Noonan, Gregory, Mikel Redman, and Scott Russell. *Brewer's Handbook.* Ann Arbor, Mich.: G. W. Kent, 1996.

O'Rourke, Timothy. "Yeast: Nature's Little Beer Maker." *The New Brewer* 11, no. 2 (October 1994).

———. "What Ever Happened to Maturation?" *The New Brewer* 12, no. 2 (March–April 1995).

Papazian, Charlie. *The New Complete Joy of Home Brewing.* New York: Avon Books, 1991.

———. "Yeast—The Sorcerer's Apprentice." *Zymurgy* 12, no. 4 (Special 1989).

Pasteur, Louis. *Études sur la bière.* Paris: Gauthier-Villars, 1876.

Protz, Roger. *The Ultimate Encyclopedia of Beer.* New York: Smithmark, 1995.

Rajotte, Piérre. *Belgian Ale.* Classic Beer Style Series, no. 6. Boulder, Colo.: Brewers Publications, 1992.

Randel, H. W. G. "Altbier-Herstellung Heute." *Brauwelt* 116, no. 33 (August 1976).

Reed, Gerald, and Tilak Nagodawthina. *Yeast Technology*. New York: Van Nostrand Reinhold, 1991.

Richman, Darryl. *Bock*. Classic Beer Style Series, no. 9. Boulder, Colo.: Brewers Publications, 1994.

Rümmler, Else. *Zum Uerige*—Past and Presence. 2nd ed. Düsseldorf: Josef und Christa Schnitzler, 1985.

Schloßbauverein Burg an der Wupper. *Adels Schloß und Ritter Burg*. 4th ed. Essen, Germany: Thales, 1995.

Schumann, Uwe-Jens. *Deutschland Deine Biere*. Munich: Zaber Sandmann, 1993.

Shellenberger, Diana. "A Noble Enterprise." *The New Brewer* 14, no. 1 (January–February 1997).

Sillner, Leo. *Das Buch vom Bier*. Munich: Feder-Verlag, 1962.

Sinz, Herbert. *1000 Jahre Kölsch Bier*. Puhlheim, Germany: REM, 1985.

Unios CB. *South Bohemia*. Ceske Krumlov, Czech Republic: Unios CB Co. Ltd., n.d.

Walz, Greg. "Boiling Methods and Techniques." *Zymurgy* 10, no. 5 (Winter 1987).

Warner, Eric. *German Wheat Beer*. Classic Beer Style Series, no. 7. Boulder, Colo.: Brewers Publications, 1992.

———. "The Art and Science of Decoction Mashing." *Zymurgy* 16, no. 4 (Special 1993).

———. "Malting Techniques." *Zymurgy* 16, no. 4 (Special 1993).

———. "An Overview of the German Brewing History." *Zymurgy* 16, no. 4 (Special 1993).

Picture Credits

■ ■

Permission for use of the following photographs is gratefully acknowledged:

Photo of early "cold machines," page 74, and of Hoepfner Brewery's pile of ice, page 86. Courtesy of Privatbrauerei Hoepfner, Karlsruhe, Germany. Photo of twelfth-century brewery, page 50. Courtesy of Holsten-Brauerei AG, Hamburg, Germany. Photo of German men, page xi. Courtesy of Uerige Obergärige Hausbrauerei GmbH, Düsseldorf, Germany. From *Kölsch Bier- und Brauhäuser*, by Franz Mathar and Rudolf Spiegel. Engraving of Emperor Maximilian I, page 53, photo of wooden statue of Gambrinus, page 59, and engraving of Cologne, page 60. Copyright 1989 by Greven Verlag, Cologne, Germany. Courtesy of the publisher. From *German Wheat Beer*, by Eric Warner. Photo of weisse glass, page 113. Copyright 1992 by Brewers Publications. Courtesy of the publisher. Photo of German tribesmen, page 13 (top left). Used by permission of Bildarchiv Preußischer Kulturbesitz, Berlin, Germany. Photos of labels, pages 3, 6, 12, 45, 47, 64 (all), 69, 70 (all), 71 (all), 73, 92, 96, 97 (all), 99 (all), 106, 115 (top), 116 (middle), 118 (top), 120 (bottom three), 121, 122 (top), 123 (top two), 124 (bottom). From the collection of Chuck Doughty. Used by permission. Photos of coasters, pages 1, 2 (all), 9 (top left), 28, 46, 65, 88 (top), 90, 93, 94 (all), 100, 101 (all), 106 (top), 107 (all), 108 (top two), 109 (all), 110, 111, 114, 115 (bottom), 116 (top), 118 (bottom), 119 (all), 123 (bottom). From the collection of Horst Genten. Used by permission. Photos of mugs, pages 37, 55 (all), 75, 98, by Mark Duffley. From the collection of Horst Genten. Used by permission. Photos of glass boots, page 88; two steins, page 98; glass of beer, page 108; beer bottle, page 110; wheat beer glass, page 112 (top right); glass of Pilsener, page 116; mug, page 120; bottle, page 122; bottle, page 124; and author photo, page 147, by Mark Duffley. Used by permission of the photographer. Photo of the entrance gate to the city of Lübeck, page 60, by Darryl Richman. Used by permission of the photographer. Photo of medieval map of Europe, page 8. Engraving from Sebastian Müntzer, *Cosmographia Universalis,* lib. vi, Basel 1500–1504; by permission of the Bodleian Library, University of Oxford, Great Britian. Photos of the sign for Historischer Ratskeller, page 3, wood carving of brew monk, page 5; Kulmbach Mönchshof, page 9; flute concert in Frederick II's salon in Berlin, page 89; and Uerige brewpub sign, page 105, by Horst Dornbusch. Used by permission of the photographer. Photos of Düsseldorf's coat of arms and Düsseldorf in 1585, page 57, and a beer wagon, page 63. From the collection of Horst Dornbusch. Used by permission.

About the Author

Horst Dornbusch was born and raised in Düsseldorf, Germany, the home of Germany's most famous ale, the alt beer.

In 1969, Horst came to the United States on a Fulbright Grant. He earned a B.A. from Reed College in sociology and an M.A. from Brandeis University in politics. He worked for two decades in journalism and publishing, writing radio news for the Canadian Broadcasting Corporation in Montreal, editing books for the *Reader's Digest* in Montreal, and managing the technical publications department of Siemens Medical Electronics in Danvers, Massachusetts.

Disappointed by the beers he found in America, he decided to become a homebrewer and make his own. He also began studying the standard texts of German master brewer programs and enlisted as a "brewpie"—a volunteer week-end apprentice—at the Ipswich Brewing Company in Massachusetts, where he learned to make beer on a commercial scale. In 1995 he turned what he had learned about brewing into a commercial enterprise and founded the Dornbusch Brewing Company, Inc., a contract brewery specializing in German-style microbrewed beers. In his spare time he combines his love of beer and words by lecturing and writing about brewing and the appreciation of beer.